Global

Intercessory Prayer

Study Guide

by David L. Finnell

Published by DLF Ministries
134 Point South Lane
Lexington, SC 29073
U.S.A.

Printed in the Republic of Singapore
by BAC Printers

This intercessory prayer guide

is dedicated to my wife,

Linda,

whose constant and unconditional love for

God, myself, and others has shown me how to love.

About the Author

David Finnell, a graduate of Southwestern Baptist Theological Seminary, served as a foreign missionary of the Southern Baptist Convention from 1978-1988. Serving in the country of Singapore, he was the director of the Baptist Centre for Urban Studies, which was responsible for a church planting and evangelistic strategy for Singapore. He also served as an evangelistic research consultant, evangelist, and church planter. Following a lengthy illness, Dr. Finnell is now teaching in the areas of evangelism, prayer, and church planting at Columbia Bible College and Seminary in Columbia, South Carolina. Dr. Finnell is also serving as Director of the International Network of Church Planters. He is married to the former Miss Linda Lipscomb of Jackson, Mississippi. They have two sons, Shane (14) & Nathan (10).

Purpose

The purpose of this book is to equip believers with a powerful prayer life to empower the body of Christ to complete the mission of Christ to redeem mankind. This book was written (1) for missionaries to use to build powerful prayer support for their ministries, (2) for mission minded churches to use to build a powerful global prayer ministry, and (3) to help individuals to begin and maintain a personal ministry of global intercessory prayer. It may be particularly useful to provide a meaningful and purposeful ministry to retirees, individuals who are converted while in prison, and individuals who are severely handicapped or homebound.

Individual Study

By reading and completing the activities in this book, the reader can develop a powerful intercessory prayer life. It is very important that you complete all activities, don't just read the book! Reading alone will not change your prayer life! It is extremely important that you set up your prayer notebook and commit yourself to the eight week prayer diary.

Small Group Study

For small group study, participants should complete one chapter each week through personal study and use the **For Group Discussions** at the end of each chapter as a guide for their class session. The ideal time for each class period is 90 minutes. Chapter One should be completed before the first class. The length of the course should be 12 or 13 weeks. Each of the chapters on Power Builders and Drainers will require two weeks each to cover the material. Each person using this book should order a copy of *Operation World*. If your class sessions are 90 minutes in length, consider showing the video entitled *The Role of Prayer in Spiritual Awakenings* by J. Edwin Orr during the session on Prayer and Revival.

Table of Contents

Chapter One
Testimonies of Prayer

Jesus was a man of prayer. Throughout the Gospels, we see the emphasis Jesus placed on prayer: *And after He had sent the multitudes away, He went up to the mountain by Himself to pray; and when it was evening, He was there alone* (Matthew 14:23). *And after bidding them farewell, He departed to the mountain to pray* (Mark 6:46). *But He Himself would often slip away to the wilderness and pray* (Luke 5:16). *And it was at this time that He went off to the mountain to pray, and He spent the whole night in prayer to God* (Luke 6:12).

If we truly want to learn to pray, we need to ask Jesus to teach us to pray. In The Prayer Life, Andrew Murray writes:

> *I had not supposed that just as He* (Jesus) *will give all other grace in answer to prayer, so above all and before all, He will bestow the grace of a praying heart. What folly to think that all other blessings must come from Him, but that prayer, whereon everything else depends, must be obtained by personal effort. Thank God I began to comprehend - the Lord Jesus is Himself in the inner chamber watching over me, and holding Himself responsible to teach me how to approach the Father.*

Prepare yourself for this study with prayer.

- **Give praise to God, confess your sins before God, and pray for the power of the Holy Spirit to work through your life.**

- **Prepare yourself to be sensitive to the leadership of the Holy Spirit for revelation, instruction, and direction.**

- **Ask Jesus to teach you to pray. Ask Him to give you a burden to pray.**

Put your book down and pray.

1

The following is a personal testimony of the author, David Finnell, of the power of intercessory prayer.

In the summer of 1968, I went to the Mississippi gulf coast to a large Baptist camp to spend the summer as a counselor. Over 100 college students from all over the state worked at the camp during the summer. There were jobs for counselors, lifeguards, maintenance personnel, and cafeteria workers, to name a few. It was such a large group of

people, that the staffers lived in another camp about two miles down the coast. In order to get a job as a staffer, you had to get a recommendation from your church that you were a hard worker and a good, moral Christian. The supervision at the staffer's camp was limited, so it was important that the staffers be screened to supposedly prevent immoral conduct at the camp.

As a counselor, I spent the weekdays at the main camp and went to the staffer's camp only on the weekend. Thus I really didn't develop a lot of friends, other than fellow counselors, and didn't get into a lot of the social events and cliques among the staffers. Besides, I had just discovered that my parents were getting a divorce and was somewhat anti-social at the time.

About the third weekend, five people approached me at the staffer's camp. They wanted to talk in private, so we went into my room. They shared with me about the horrible moral situation among the staffers. There was smoking, drinking, partying, and a lot of pairing off of couples with no supervision. The place was spiritually dead and was becoming a den of sin. They had talked with the camp parents, but the parents thought these young people were overreacting. Somehow these staffers had been led to me. Why, I'll never know apart from Providence. I probably stood apart from what was going on, but not from any reason of spirituality. But the group felt that I might somehow give them some advice.

Advice? From me?

Who was I to offer advice to a group of young adults who were older and probably more mature than I? But at their insistence, I made a few suggestions, and prayed for them during the week.

When I returned to the staffer's camp the following week, the group approached me again. They had taken my advice, and things had only gotten worse. But they again felt led to seek some more ideas or advice from me. This was incredible. I certainly was sympathetic to the group, but how could they return to a stranger whose advice was so pitiful?

Then it came to me! It was so clear a revelation, there could be no doubt as to its source. I asked them if they truly had a burden to see a revival break out among the campers. They all agreed. Then I told them, if they truly wanted revival, to get on their knees in prayer as a group, and stay on their knees until the burden was lifted. Their faces changed expressions. For the first time, their looks of hope turned sour. What good could this bring? They had felt this burden for weeks; how long would they have to pray?

"Until the burden is gone," I responded.

"Through the night?" they asked.

"Until the burden is gone."

"What about meals?"

"Until the burden is gone," I responded.

This was crazy! They said they'd have to think about it and left quite disappointed.

A short while later, the group returned. They asked if I would join them in this prayer marathon. After making the suggestion, how could I refuse? So we went into my room at 2:00 p.m. on Friday afternoon, got on our knees and began to pray. At first it was a little awkward. What all do you pray for in such a marathon? But after expressing our prayers for the burden of revival, the Holy Spirit began to convict us of our own sin. That was not a part of our bargain, but after the cleansing, that little prayer group was full of the Holy Spirit, and it was a thrilling experience.

Supper passed. Eight o'clock passed. We prayed on. Midnight passed. Then at two o'clock in the morning, I sensed that we needed to go out and get some fresh air. But before we took our break, we prayed that God would give us some indication that we were on the right track, and not just going through some dramatic and emotional exercise.

When we left my room, the cool night air refreshed our tired and aching bodies. Praying for so long in a rustic dorm room is a cramping experience in more ways than one. I still remember the sound of the ocean waves beating on the beach only 150 yards away. But before we had taken ten steps, we heard a door slam about ten doors down. A fellow staffer walked eagerly toward us and demanded that we talk with him. He was obviously in some distress, so we all sat down right there in the grass. He shared how that afternoon the Lord started convicting him of how sinful he had been there at camp, and he had wrestled with it all night. He just couldn't get to sleep. We counseled with him, and he rededicated his life anew to Christ. We asked him if he could remember what time he started coming under conviction. The best he could remember, it must have been around 2:30 that afternoon.

It was like a sign from heaven. Shortly we returned to my room and began praying. Then, all of a sudden, there was a silence. We all looked up and wondered if the others had felt the same emotion. Then we joyously confirmed it: the burden was gone. Revival had already begun. We prayed several prayers of praise, and soon our prayer session was over.

The next morning, revival had broken out even before we got up. In the next few days, several were saved, and many young people rededicated their lives to Christ. The camp of sin had turned into a camp of righteousness. God had shown us how revival takes place. He had also shown us the power of intercessory prayer.

Answer the following questions about this testimony:

1. What were the moral conditions of the camp during the third weekend?

2. What was the prayer group asking God to do?

3. At what point in time was the group's prayer answered?

4. Was the revival that took place dependent upon the group members physically spreading the word about a need for repentance and revival?

5. Who brought about the revival and spread it through the camp?

6. Have you ever prayed in this way? Why or why not?

A Friend's Testimony

Select a member of your church or a Christian friend whom you believe to be a person of prayer. Ask them to give you a personal testimony of God's answering their prayers. Write a summary of that testimony in the space provided.

Your Testimony of Answered Prayer

Write the most powerful testimony of answered prayer in your life. Clearly state the way in which you interceded, your expectations (positive or negative), the answer, and your feelings concerning the answered prayer.

Do not begin Chapter Two until all activities in Chapter One are completed.

For Group Discussions

1. Open with a time of prayer.

2. Remind each student the importance of completing all assignments before each class. If the class is larger than ten, break down into groups of four to complete activities three through six.

3. Ask each class member to share their name, favorite Scripture verse, and a personal testimony of answered prayer.

4. Review the questions on pages five through six concerning the author's testimony.

5. Ask each class member to share the testimony of the person they interviewed.

6. Spend the remaining time in group prayer. Allow each person an opportunity to pray about their participation in this course, the growth of their own prayer lives, and for the prayer life of their congregation.

ASSIGNMENT: Complete Chapter Two by the next class meeting. If you failed to complete any activities in Chapter One, complete them by the next class.

Chapter Two
Prayer Analysis

Preparation

Prepare yourself for this chapter with prayer. Give praise to God, confess your sins before God, and pray for the power of the Holy Spirit to work through your life. Prepare yourself to be sensitive to the leadership of the Holy Spirit for revelation, instruction, and direction.

Before the Throne

When we pray to God, we are coming directly to the throne of the God of the Universe in all His majesty, power, and glory. Yet we know that God is ready and waiting to commune with us through prayer. When we think about the awesome reality of such an encounter, it is marvelous to know that He waits upon us and desires to fellowship with us. The drawing on the next page is a visual description of one of the ways we can view the reality of prayer. In the space below, describe your interpretation of this little drawing in light of prayer.

10

The previous illustration alone does not give us a balanced perspective of prayer. Prayer involves a paradox in that it is an awesome experience of coming before our glorious and majestic God. Yet in spite of the awesomeness of prayer, through prayer we are brought into an intimate and close fellowship with our mighty creator. It is often hard for us to imagine that such a powerful and mighty God can be so approachable and desires to fellowship with each of His children as He walked and talked with Adam and Eve in the garden. So in spite of the greatness of God, through prayer we are brought into the inner circle to fellowship.

Some people are too fearful of such a mighty God to be comfortable in approaching Him in an intimate way. We are not to be fearful of God in the sense of being afraid. Our fear of God should entail respect, reverence, and awe. Many people cautiously approach God, not wanting to bother Him, then dial in the special code (Dear Heavenly Father), close their eyes, and deliver their petitions as if they were communicating over a one-way telephone line.

Another misconception of prayer is to view prayer as a duty. Prayer that is perceived as a duty is a burden. Powerful prayer is not sourced in our duty. It is a glorious, wonderful, and joyful relationship. In spite of the awesomeness of who we are talking with, prayer is an intimate relationship. Too many times we think of our prayer life as that time which begins with "Dear Heavenly Father," and ends with "Amen." But with a lifestyle of prayer, we can commune with God with our eyes open, while driving the car, while eating a meal, while working, before making any decision, before meeting a new person, or any other time so that we can know God's will for our lives in all things.

To truly understand what prayer is, we must balance the illustration on the previous page with the illustration of relationship on the following page. Study the illustration on the next page. In light of these two illustrations, and the discussion on this page, how would you describe your own prayer life? Write your response below.

When we begin to grasp prayer as a relationship, we begin to grow in our relationship to God and to His Son, Jesus. But before we begin the process of growth, it would be helpful to consider where you presently are in your prayer life. Since there is no accurate way to measure something as subjective as your relationship to God, we will measure your prayer life by considering what you are praying for.

Personal Prayer Analysis

The fact that you are reading this book indicates a desire to become a global prayer intercessor. But before you learn to become a global prayer intercessor, you must discover where you presently are in terms of global intercessory prayer. To do this, take the following test. For each question, give yourself the points indicated based upon your response. For question number one, if you have a personal prayer and Bible study time every day, give yourself 10 points. Write the number of points you receive for each question on the blank space to the right of the question. When you finish, total your points, and enter the total in the space provided.

YOUR PRAYER ANALYSIS

1. How often do you have a personal prayer &
    Bible study time?   _____

Daily	10 points	Weekly	1 point
Every other day	6 points	Less than weekly	0 points
Twice a week	4 points		

2. Do you pray for the specific needs of your church staff
    and leadership?   _____

Daily	10 points
Every other day to weekly	3 points
Less than weekly	0 points

3. Do you pray for the salvation of specific individuals on a
    daily basis?   _____

10 + people	10 points	2 - 4 people	6 points
5 - 10 people	8 points	1 person	2 points
		No people	0 points

4. How often do you attend your church's regular
    prayer services?   _____

| Always | 10 points | Seldom or never | 0 points |
| Sometimes | 3 points | | |

5. Approximately how many specific items do you pray
   for each day?   _____

100 or more	10 points	21 to 50	3 points
51 to 100	7 points	5 to 19	1 point
		4 or less	0 points

6. Do you pray specifically for world missions each day? _____

   Yes   10 points   No   0 points

7. Do you pray during the invitation time (altar calls) of
   evangelistic services and rallies for people needing to
   make decisions?   _____

| Always | 10 points | Seldom or never | 0 points |
| Sometimes | 3 points | | |

8. Do you pray specifically for guidance concerning your
   personal and/or family decisions?   _____

| Always | 10 points | Seldom or never | 0 points |
| Sometimes | 3 points | | |

9. Do you pray daily for the second coming of Christ?   _____

| Always | 10 points | Seldom or never | 0 points |
| Sometimes | 3 points | | |

10. Do you pray against the work of Satan in your life
    and ministry?   _____

At least once each day	10 points
Several times a week	6 points
About once a week	2 points
Less than weekly	0 points

                                      TOTAL _____

Find your personal prayer rating from the list below.

85 to 100 points   A mighty prayer warrior
75 to 84 points   A prayer intercessor
65 to 74 points   An apprentice prayer intercessor
55 to 64 points   A weak prayer force
45 to 54 points   A neutral force in spiritual warfare
45 or less points A prayer & power liability to your church

Fill in the blank based upon your current rating:

Currently I am _____.

Don't be shocked if you are a prayer liability. A majority of people in most churches today are liabilities. Some of you are so shocked that you may argue about the validity of the test. What is the test measuring? **It is focusing on your prayer support for the completion of the mission of Christ upon the earth through His body, the local church.** The test is admittedly subjective, but it has been very helpful in demonstrating the problem of prayerlessness and the lack of power in our churches today. If your church does not meet regularly for prayer, through no fault of your own, this still has an impact upon your own personal prayer life. As for prayer for the return of Christ, this will be dealt with later in this book.

Now read a description of each of the prayer ratings to see what it indicates.

A mighty prayer warrior is a daily global prayer intercessor committed to consistent intercession on behalf of the church for great power in ministry and boldness in witnessing; a persistent global prayer warrior for the lost who prays that the power of the Holy Spirit will convict specific people of sin and draw them to Christ; a warrior against the evil one; a powerful warrior of the body of Christ, full of the Holy Spirit.

<u>A prayer intercessor</u> is a consistent global prayer intercessor; a powerful warrior for specific intercessions ranging from a personal to a global level.

<u>An apprentice prayer intercessor</u> is an individual who is growing and learning global intercessory prayer; fairly consistent in prayer.

<u>A weak prayer force</u> is an individual who considers oneself a good Christian and church member; very committed, but has limited understanding of global intercessory prayer and spiritual warfare; possibly hot and cold in their prayer life.

<u>A neutral force in spiritual warfare</u> receives the same amount of spiritual resources (power) from the church as they put into it (through prayer); they have little understanding of global intercessory prayer and spiritual warfare; they possibly have a roller coaster prayer life.

<u>A prayer and power liability to your church</u> receives more power from the church than they give to it through prayer; they are consumer oriented church attenders (joined because of what the church could do for them with little consideration of what they could do for the church); they are a power drainer in the church who are either carnal Christians or just have never been taught or challenged with spiritual warfare or global intercessory prayer; they are just as likely an active church member or leader as not.

Spend a few moments in prayer and ask the Lord what He desires your goal to be six months from now. Be realistic in setting your goal. One cannot go from being a prayer liability to a mighty prayer warrior in the blink of an eye. Such movement is a growth process.

Fill in the blank based upon your goal in prayer:

My goal is to be _____.

Church Analysis

As an individual student, it is impossible for you to accurately calculate the prayer power of your church. But for the sake of illustration, we will attempt to show the general condition of the average evangelical church.

So this illustration will be more relevant, gather the following information from your church.

What is the total membership of your church? _____

What is the average attendance at your church's regular prayer service? If your church doesn't provide an opportunity for regular corporate prayer, then the average is 0. _____

Do not continue until you have these figures. A rough estimate of these figures will be adequate for our purpose of illustration. Let's select an imaginary church called Port Arthur Community Church (PACC). Let's say this church has the same membership and average attendance in its regular prayer service as your church has.

First we must measure how many people in the church would be described as prayer warriors. Think back to the test. We must know how people would score in the top four categories: a mighty prayer warrior, a prayer intercessor, an apprentice prayer intercessor, and a weak prayer force.

You cannot assume that everyone who attends your regular prayer services are prayer warriors, but we will be generous and assume that 40% of those attending the prayer service at Port Arthur Community Church (PACC) are in the top four categories. Take the average number of people who attend the regular prayer services at PACC (the same as in your church) and multiply it times .40 (i.e. 40%). Enter the total in the space provided.

Intercessors = _____

The next category is the neutral force in spiritual power. These people receive about the same amount of ministry and prayer power from the life of the church as they put into it. Thus they do not add anything to the corporate prayer power of the church. At PACC, about 10% of the average attendance at the regular prayer service would fall into this category. Take the average number of people who attend the regular prayer services at PACC (the same as in your church) and multiply it times .10 (i.e. 10%). Enter the total in the space provided.

Neutral _____ = 0

The final category is the individuals who receive more (in terms of ministry and power) from the church than they put into it (through prayer, and thus power). To calculate this category, subtract the total number of people from the previous two categories (Intercessors and Neutral) from the total church membership. If the total membership is 600, and there are 32 people in the other categories, then the total number of liabilities are 568 (600 - 32 = 568).

Liabilities = (_____)

Now, enter the above figures in the appropriate places below. To get your total, add where it says add, and subtract where it says subtract.

Intercessors   = _____ [add]

Neutral _____   = 0

Liabilities   = (_____) [Subtract]

Total (+/-)   = _____

In order to fill in the church power meter, we need to get the percentage of the church membership. If the church membership is 600, and our rating is -536, we divide 536 by 600. This will give us a decimal figure of .89. This means 89%. But more importantly, this means a negative 89%.

If you are not mathematically oriented, and do not understand how to make the power meter calculation, please ask someone with some mathematic or accounting background to assist you.

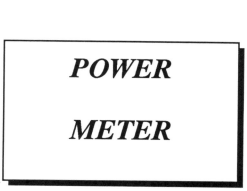

	100%
	80%
	60%
	40%
	20%
	0%
	-20%
	-40%
	-60%
	-80%
	-100%

Fill in the power meter with Port Arthur Community Church's percentage as you would a thermometer. The power meter is illustrative of the spiritual warfare going on between the church and its community (and also the world). Either the church or the community will have the most power. If the church has the most spiritual power (empowered by the Holy Spirit), it will change the community, evangelize it, and change the lives of those in it. If the community or the world has the most power (empowered by Satan), then the worldly and secular things will have more influence upon the lives of the church members than vice versa. It is all a question of spiritual power.

In light of the power meter, describe the spiritual power of Port Arthur Community Church. Is this church changing its community, or are the things of the world (including television, movies, immorality, pornography, materialism, wrong attitudes, etc.) changing and molding the church members? Write your conclusions in the space provided.

Do you think your church has more or less spiritual power than Port Arthur Community Church? Describe the spiritual power of your church in light of your community.

Closing Prayer

Spend several minutes in prayer reflecting on what you have learned in this lesson.

For Group Discussions

1. Open with a time of prayer.

2. Discuss whether group member's prayer lives are built on a relationship or out of duty.

3. Discuss the test. What is the test trying to measure? How did you score? Were you surprised with your score? Why or why not?

4. Discuss the prayer ratings. What are the implications of these ratings for evangelism and ministry?

5. Share your calculation of Port Authur Community Church's prayer power. Do you think your church has more or less power than PACC? Help any students who do not understand how to calculate the power meter.

6. Calculate the power meter for your class. Discuss the implications. Add up the number of class members in each category. Enter the group figures in the appropriate places below. To get your total, add where it says add, and subtract where it says subtract.

Intercessors   = _____ [add]

Neutral _____   =   0

Liabilities   = (_____) [Subtract]

Total (+/-)   =   _____

Fill in the power meter on the next page based upon your class score.

CLASS POWER METER

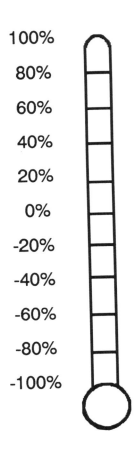

100%

80%

60%

40%

20%

0%

-20%

-40%

-60%

-80%

-100%

6. Spend the remaining time in prayer as a group. Ask the Lord to give each individual and the group a prayerful heart. Spend time in intercession for one another, and for the prayer life of your church.

ASSIGNMENT: Complete Chapter Three by the next class meeting.

Chapter Three
Steps 1 - 5 of
Global Intercessory Prayer

Preparation

Prepare yourself for this session with prayer. Give praise to God, confess your sins before God, and pray for the power of the Holy Spirit to work through your life. Prepare yourself to be sensitive to the leadership of the Holy Spirit for revelation, instruction, and direction. There are 14 steps to global intercessory prayer. In this chapter, we will be studying the first five steps.

STEP ONE: Praise & Thanksgiving

Begin your intercessory time with a season (time) of praise. One of the meaningful ways to praise God is to select a psalm and pray it in the first person, present tense. For example, *I will extol Thee, my God, O King,* easily changes to *I extol You, my God, O King* by taking out the word *will.* You also substitute *He* or *the Lord* with *YOU* since you are talking directly to God. *Praise Him for His mighty deeds* becomes *I praise You for Your mighty deeds.* After a little practice, it becomes very natural and meaningful. Some psalms can be prayed without any changes. Try praying Psalm 139, not just reading it, but praying it. Other psalms that may lend themselves to prayers of praise are 23, 67, 98, 143, 145, 146, 147, 148, and 150. There are many others. In your praise time, prepare for intercession by humbling yourself before God and acknowledging who He is in all His glory and the relationship you have with Him through Jesus Christ, His Son. It's a time for worship, adoration, and thanksgiving. Thanksgiving should permeate your entire prayer time. It is a part of praise, but you also give thanks for each answered prayer.

Another way to praise God during your prayer time is to sing praises to Him. This does not include singing songs about God, but songs or choruses that are directed *to* Him. When I sing "Father I Adore You," I am telling the Father of my adoration of Him. When I sing songs such as the doxology, I am singing a song about praise. There is a big difference between singing about God, and singing to God. Songs during our prayer time are not true prayers unless we are singing them to God in the first person.

> Take time now to praise God and give thanks to Him in your own words; then pray Psalm 139.

STEP TWO: Confession

Now is the time for cleansing; for the removal of any unconfessed sin that may stand in the way of your communication channel with God. As you confess your sins, consider each of the following areas, search your heart and mind, and confess any sins that the Holy Spirit reveals to you.

- **Sins of the Flesh** - are the sins described in the Ten Commandments, and others such as drinking, gambling, etc. These are the bad things that we normally think of when we think of sin.

- **Sins of the Spirit** - are wrong attitudes or relationships concerning God, men, or things. Jesus was more concerned about these sins than sins of the flesh. But today, we would welcome the Pharisees before we would even speak to the woman at the well. In your confession time, place an emphasis on this area. To the committed Christian, this area will hinder the power of our prayer life more than any other, because we don't easily recognize the sins of the Spirit and don't confess them to God.

- **Sins of Omission** - are things you should have done, but didn't. If you miss your prayer time, Bible study, or fail to witness when an opportunity is there, don't sit there with a guilty heart. Confess the sin and look forward.

Prayerlessness is sin. Many times we think of prayer as a privilege rather than a responsibility. Paul says we are to *devote ourselves to prayer* (Colossians 4:2). Throughout Scripture we are called upon

24

to pray. Samuel recognized if He failed on his responsibility to pray, it was a sin: *Moreover, as for me, far be it from me that I should sin against the Lord by ceasing to pray for you;* (1 Samuel 12:23a). When we fail to pray, we are sinning against the Lord.

● **Unconscious Sins** - are things we do without realizing they displease God. We all have sin in this category. Pray for forgiveness and ask the Holy Spirit to reveal these hidden sins to you. Then He will do so when you are ready to deal with them. But don't dwell on this and let it be a burden.

There should be joy in the confession of sin as the burden of guilt is removed and we can focus on the future rather than the past.

> Take time now to confess your sins before God in prayer. Confess sins in each of the four categories. Claim 1 John 1:9. "If we confess our sins, He is faithful and righteous to forgive our sins and to cleanse us from all unrighteousness."

STEP THREE - Spiritual
Preparation For The Day

Spiritual preparation for the day must naturally be in the morning, but your petition time can be at any convenient time. Following are some prayers that can help you to live a more righteous life if you pray, claim, and follow them on a daily basis. A righteous life is necessary for a powerful prayer life. *"The effective prayer of a righteous man can accomplish much."* James 5:16.

⟹ First - Filling of the Spirit.

Once we have emptied ourselves of unconfessed sin, we need to fill up that space with the Holy Spirit. Being filled with the Spirit is not automatic, we must ask for it through prayer each day.

> In your own words, pray this prayer: Dear Heavenly Father, fill me with your Holy Spirit today.

⟹ Second - Bear the fruit of the Spirit.

Now that we have been filled with the Spirit, we need to make a specific request of what we want the Spirit to do in our lives today - something which is natural for the Spirit and against our nature in the flesh - that something which will enable us to live a righteous and joyful life. The fruit of the Spirit can be ours each day if we will just ask for it. You can have joy in your life on a daily basis if you will just ask for the Spirit to bear that fruit in your life each day. It can be done by praying and claiming Galatians 5:22. As you list each fruit, consciously consider relevant areas of need in your life for the coming day. Meditate on each fruit and claim it!

Pray Galatians 5:22: Dear Heavenly Father, bear the fruit of Thy Spirit in my life today. Bear the fruit of love, joy, peace, patience, kindness, goodness, faithfulness, gentleness, and self-control....

⟹ Third - Claim Christ in me.

The next great need in preparation for the day is the problem of self. We must daily deny self and place Christ on the throne of our lives. This can be done by praying and claiming Galatians 2:20.

Dear Father, I want to claim today that I am crucified with Christ, it is no longer I who live, but Christ lives in me. And the life I now live in the flesh this day, I live by faith in the Son of God, who loves me and delivered Himself up for me.

⟹ Fourth - Claim Romans 8:28.

It has been very helpful for me to claim Romans 8:28 each day in prayer. Doing so accomplishes three things: (1) it builds confidence in God no matter what the circumstances, (2) provides an opportunity to affirm my love to God, and (3) causes me to pray that I will discern and then follow God's will for my life on a daily basis.

It is very important that we express ourselves to those we love. When was the last time you actually told God that you love Him? To tell Him of your love is an act of praise and worship. Tell Him you love Him each and every day.

> Dear Father, I want to claim your promise that all things work together for good to those who love You, to those called according to Your purpose. I love You, Lord, with all my heart and pray that I will be in the center of Your perfect will today.

⟹ Fifth - Protection from Satan.

A prayer intercessor is a warrior against Satan, and, to be sure, Satan declares war against all prayer intercessors. In the Lord's prayer, we are taught to pray for protection from the Evil One. It is the Lord who protects us. If Michael the Archangel was not willing to personally attack Satan, then neither should we. Michael said, "The Lord rebuke you Satan!" (Jude 9), and the battle was won. David used the same phrase in the Psalms. Jesus quoted Scripture when He was attacked by Satan. Let's follow that example.

> Dear Father, protect my family and me from the Evil One today. "The Lord rebuke you, Satan!"

⇨ Sixth - Thy Kingdom Come.

The Scripture teaches us to pray for the second coming of Christ. In the Lord's prayer, He taught us to pray, *Thy kingdom come.* Since this is the prayer Christ gave to us for our instruction in the 20th Century as well as for the disciples, Jesus meant not only for the disciples to pray for the ushering in of the kingdom at the resurrection, but also for the consummation of the kingdom at the second coming. Jesus knew His model prayer would be the only model He would give to us in His Holy Scripture. Then surely He intended for us to pray *Thy kingdom come* even today.

The disciples understood that they were to pray *Thy kingdom come* following the resurrection. Paul and John prayed for the second coming. We find that Paul prayed for the second coming when he prayed *maranatha*, which means *O, our Lord come.* (1 Cor 16:22).

The second to last verse of the Bible is a prayer of John for the second coming of Christ (*Come, Lord Jesus.* Rev 22:20b). Also in the Revelation of John, the prayers of the saints are repeatedly mentioned in relation to the second coming (Rev 5:8; 8:3). Although these prayers are not specifically identified as prayers for the second coming, an argument can be made for such a relationship. Christ taught us to pray for His return; Scripture shows that the disciples prayed for His return; and Scripture's portrayal of the events in heaven surrounding His return refer to the prayers of the saints. Why would these prayers even be mentioned if not for their relevancy to the context? The context of these prayers are the end of the age and the return of Christ.

Peter taught us that "*the end of all things is at hand, therefore be of sound judgement and sober spirit for the purpose of prayer*" (1 Peter 4:7). This passage is not a prayer for the second coming, but indicates the importance of prayer to the end time. Peter also tells us we should be "*looking for and hastening the coming of the day of God, on account of which the heavens will be destroyed by burning, and the elements will melt with intense heat!*" (2 Peter 3:12). This means that we should be expecting, hastening, and earnestly desiring Christ's return. How do we hasten Christ's return? By working to complete Christ's mission on earth through our actions and prayers.

There is even evidence of praying for the return of Christ in the Old Testament: *On your walls, O Jerusalem, I have appointed watchmen; all day and all night they will never keep silent. You who remind the Lord, take no rest for yourselves; and give Him no rest until He establishes and makes Jerusalem a praise in the earth* (Isaiah 62: 6-7). How do we remind the Lord? We do it through prayer. We are to pray continually, giving God no rest, until Jerusalem is established as a light for the salvation of the world. The context here is the end of the age and the consummation of the Kingdom of God. Through the revelation of the New Testament, we know this consummation will occur at Christ's return. A careful study of Isaiah 60-66 sheds much light on this passage.

When I pray for the second coming, I pray also for the fulfillment of the prophecy of global evangelization which will precede the second coming (Matt. 24:14). These two prayers are virtually synonymous.

Some may argue that we shouldn't pray for the second coming of Christ because of the sovereignty of God. Christ will return according to God's timing. But the issue here is not whether or not or even when Christ will return. The issue is whether or not we will be a part of it through prayer. He taught us to pray for His return. He will move us to pray for His return. Then He will return.

> Dear Father, I pray for the second coming of my Lord and Savior Jesus Christ. I want to also pray for the fulfillment of the prophecy that every tongue on earth shall hear the Good News of Jesus Christ.

This would be a great time to include prayer for evangelistic thrusts such as Bold Mission Thrust or AD 2000.

There may be other promises of God or areas of spiritual preparation that would enhance your daily prayer time. Write it (or them) in the form of a prayer in the space provided. Pray it on a daily basis.

_____

_____

_____

_____

_____

_____

_____

This completes Step Three of Global Intercessory Prayer.

STEP FOUR - Prayer For Global Missions

A prayer intercessor is an ambassador for Christ on a global basis. You can pray for all the countries of the world. Select a resource book to use as a prayer guide and pray for one to three countries each day on a rotating basis. The best resource is *Operation World*. You may also use other resources. Don't forget to pray for countries where there is no mission work.

Using *Operation World* or an atlas, pray right now for a country of your own choosing.

STEP FIVE - Prayer For Specific Countries

You are about to become a prayer missionary assigned to two or more specific countries. Choose your countries well, for they should be part of a lifelong commitment. Select one country with an active Christian witness and learn as much as possible about its prayer needs, using the resources listed in Appendix A, newspapers, magazines, *Operation World*, etc. Create a prayer list and pray specifically for this country and its work on a daily basis.

Secondly, select a country that is closed to mission work and/or the Gospel. Research this country, its people, and its history of Christian witness. Create a prayer list. Pray daily for open doors to missionaries and the freedom of Christians to proclaim Christ. Pray against the powers of darkness who are in control of your selected country. Ask the Lord to rebuke the work of Satan in that country. Some current countries where there is no resident mission work include Vietnam, and North Korea. You can also consider adopting a country that forbids an open witness of Jesus Christ. Many Muslim countries are in this category.

Number your requests and put the date the request originated. Use the KEYWORD concept to write your requests. Here is an example.

No.   Date   Prayer Requests   Date Answered
1.   (4/16) Roger Capps - Seminary / New director / Furlough

Translated, this means a prayer request for missionary Roger Capps; for his work as director of a seminary; that a new national director may be found to take his place; for the Capps as they prepare for a furlough in America.

Using KEYWORDS can simplify your prayer lists and speed up your prayer time. We think much faster than we read, so keywords can remind us of the prayer items without having to read them verbatim from our list. Reading long prayer lists can be very tiresome and boring. Our minds also tend to wander. KEYWORDS can also easily be changed or marked as answered.

Use a pencil to make your prayer lists. When prayers are answered, enter the date to the right of the request. Leave the answered prayer on your list for a week or two as an item of praise. Then you may erase the item to make room for new requests.

On the next two pages, select two countries for the purpose of making sample prayer lists. These do not have to be your permanent selections. Use *Operation World*, resources from Appendix A, news events, etc. to write out prayer requests for these two countries.

After you complete your prayer lists for two countries, pray through those prayer lists.

Prayer for a country
WITHOUT Mission Work

Name of Country _____

No. Date Prayer Requests   Date Answered

1. (/) _____

_____

_____

_____

_____

_____

_____

_____

_____

_____

_____

_____

_____

_____

_____

_____

_____

_____

_____

_____

_____

_____

_____

_____

Prayer for a country
WITH Mission Work

Name of Country _____

No. Date Prayer Requests

Date Answered

1. (/) _____

_____

_____

_____

_____

_____

_____

_____

_____

_____

_____

_____

_____

_____

_____

_____

_____

_____

_____

_____

For Group Discussions

1. Open with a time of prayer.

2. Review the first five steps to Global Intercessory Prayer. Pay particular attention to the types of sin and to the section on Spiritual Preparation for the Day.

3. Ask each student to prepare themselves spiritually for each day for the remainder of the course.

4. Ask class members to share the countries they have chosen. Discuss different kinds of specific prayer items that may be appropriate to pray for in regards to each country. Use current news, *Operation World*, and mission magazines/newsletters as resources.

5. Review next week's assignments, then spend the remaining time in prayer. Continue to pray for one another, for the countries chosen, and for your church.

ASSIGNMENT: Complete your spiritual preparation for each day. Pray for your two countries. Spend extra time in prayers of praise and confession. Read Chapter Four. Ask students to decide which size prayer notebook they would like to use for their prayer lists. Ask students to purchase a notebook and bring it to the next class session. They should also purchase index tabs and notebook paper to fit their notebook.

Chapter Four
Steps 6 - 14 of
Global Intercessory Prayer

Preparation

Prepare yourself for this chapter with prayer. Give praise to God, confess your sins before God, and pray for the power of the Holy Spirit to work through your life. Prepare yourself to be sensitive to the leadership of the Holy Spirit for revelation, instruction, and direction.

Purchase a looseleaf notebook in order to create your prayer notebook. You may want to get a notebook the size of your Bible. This would usually be 5 1/2" by 8 1/2". You may want a smaller notebook to carry in your purse or coat pocket such as 3" by 5". You will also need to purchase some tabs. If you have the 5 1/2" by 8 1/2" notebook, you can purchase a set of 8 tab sheets. Tabs for the smaller notebooks are usually hard to find, but you can purchase stick-on tabs to create your own tab sheets or just use 3" by 5" index cards. Scissors and a hole puncher may be needed to create your notebook.

Creating Your Notebook

Once you have your looseleaf binder, you will need 8 tab sheets to organize your prayer lists. For the smaller binders, purchase 8 stick-on tabs and place them on the edges of eight 3" by 5" index cards. Another alternative is to just use the index cards by themselves. Usually 3" by 5" index cards are larger than the paper that fits 3" by 5" looseleaf binders. If necessary, punch holes in the cards to fit your notebook.

Cut out the tab labels that are included on the very last page of the book. Cut them out with some blank space on top of each word, so they can be folded. Fold the paper and place the 'Daily' tab label in the first tab sheet. Place the 'Monday' tab label in the second tab sheet, place the 'Tuesday' tab in the third tab sheet, and so on for the entire week. If you use 3" by 5" index cards without tabs, type or write the labels on the edges of the index cards.

Following each tab sheet should be 7 pages for your prayer lists *(You will learn the title for each page during this chapter.)* You may use notebook paper, or photocopy the prayer lists in Appendix B.

• The first page of your prayer notebook should be the prayer 'Checklist' in Appendix B.

• Now the remainder of your prayer notebook will include the 'DAILY' tab sheet followed by 7 prayer lists as shown below, then the 'Monday' tab sheet followed by the 7 prayer lists, then the 'Tuesday' tab sheet, followed by the 7 prayer lists, etc., for each day of the week until Sunday.

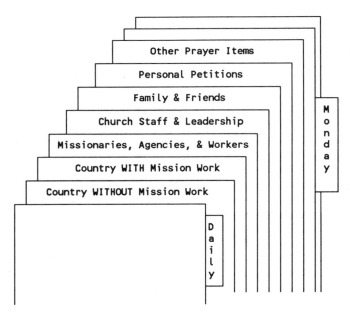

Let's review the organization of your prayer notebook again:
Following the 'Daily' tab sheet and set of seven prayer lists, insert the 'Monday' tab sheet. After the 'Monday' tab sheet should also be one

of each of the seven categories of prayer lists. Follow the same procedure for each day of the week.

Let's review it again one more time to make sure you understand: Your finished prayer notebook should include the prayer "Checklist," followed by a tab sheet marked 'Daily' for your daily prayer lists. Your daily prayer list will include each of the prayer lists you will learn to use in this chapter. As your daily list grows, you can add pages as needed in different categories. As your lists continue to grow, you can select certain items to include as weekly prayer items. You will have a tab sheet with the same seven prayer sheets for each day of the week. In the beginning, you may not have many items on your weekly list. But as you begin to pray for more and more items, you will find that there is much more to pray for than you can possibly have time. At this point, keep your priority prayer items for your daily prayers, and place other prayer items on one of your weekly lists.

Steps Six through Ten of Global Intercessory Prayer

Steps six through ten involve praying through our remaining five prayer lists on a daily basis. Let's practice making prayer lists in each of these categories.

STEP SIX - PRAYER FOR MISSIONARIES, AGENCIES, & WORKERS

List requests for specific mission agencies such as the Foreign Mission Board of the SBC, Mission to the World, Wycliffe Translators, OMF, WorldTeam, Greater Europe Mission, WEC International, etc. Pray for specific missionaries that are not from your selected country, and pray for the specific needs of these missionaries. Pray for their work, witness, joy, visas, finances, safety and protection from the Evil One, families, relationships with nationals, etc. Pray for key workers of mission agencies by name and needs each day. During this part of your prayer time you may want to pray for specific missionaries using additional resources such as birthday lists or newsletters.

In the space below, list specific requests for
selected missionaries, agencies, and agency
workers.

No. Date Prayer Requests   Date Answered

1. (/)_____

_____

_____

_____

_____

_____

_____

_____

STEP SEVEN - PRAYER FOR YOUR
CHURCH, STAFF, & LEADERS

Pray for your church staff by specific needs. Pray for the deacons,
elders, Sunday School teachers, cell group leaders, and other church
leaders. Pray for the needs of members. Pray for the right decisions
to be made by your church. Pray for unity, spiritual growth,
evangelism, ministry, etc. If your church has a weekly prayer service,
bring your notebook and take notes of prayer needs. There will be a
direct relationship between your church's collective intercessory
prayers in this section and the power available for the work of your
church. The power needed for revival, righteous living, breaking down

40

barriers of Satan in the church and community, and power for evangelism.

> In the space below, list specific requests for the needs of your church staff, leadership, selected members, coming events, evangelistic thrusts, decisions, etc.

No. Date Prayer Requests   Date Answered

1. (/)

STEP EIGHT - PRAYER FOR FAMILY & FRIENDS

Pray for your extended family by name and specific needs. *Pray specifically for unsaved family, friends, and others to whom you have the opportunity to witness.*

In the space below, list the names of selected family members with specific prayer requests. List the names of unsaved friends, neighbors, and acquaintances.

No. Date Prayer Requests   Date Answered

1. (/) _____

_____

_____

_____

_____

_____

_____

_____

_____

STEP NINE - PERSONAL PETITIONS

List all your personal petitions, needs, desires, questions, etc. Seek guidance for the decisions you make on both a large and small scale. Ask Jesus to teach you to pray and give you a prayerful heart each and every day.

In the space below, list specific personal requests.

No. Date Prayer Requests   Date Answered

1. (/   ) _____

_____

_____

_____

_____

_____

_____

_____

_____

STEP TEN - OTHER PRAYER ITEMS

List all other miscellaneous prayer items here. These might include such items as the government, the president, judicial rulings, important legislation, community needs, countries, etc. I also pray for things like: victims of world disasters to draw people to Jesus Christ, drug traffickers to be brought to justice, evil leaders to be removed from power, etc.

In the space below, list specific requests for other prayer needs in areas that God has placed upon your heart.

No. Date Prayer Requests   Date Answered

1. (/) _____

_____

_____

_____

_____

_____

_____

_____

STEP ELEVEN - PRAYERFUL
SCRIPTURE READING

In an attitude of prayer, allow the Holy Spirit to speak to you through your daily Bible readings. Read in expectation of God speaking to you in areas where there is need in your life.

STEP TWELVE - PRAYERFUL MEDITATION

Spend a few moments in meditation on your Scripture reading, prayer time, and your coming day. Include any devotional readings at this time. During your prayer time, make out a list of things you need to accomplish during the day. Check the items of priority for the day. Include items from the previous day that were not accomplished.

Spend some time listening to what God may want to bring to your heart and mind. Many times we fail to know God's will because we never pause to listen.

STEP THIRTEEN - FAMILY PRAYER

The family that prays together, stays together. If you are married, you should begin every morning with a time of prayer with your spouse. Each morning, my wife Linda and I spend a few moments sharing what we are going to do for the coming day, and then pray for one another. As a family, prayer times are very important. They don't have to be long, but your children will be taught more about prayer through what you do than by what you say. This also gives your family the opportunity to share needs, and support one another by taking your requests and concerns before God and then seeing the answers to those prayers.

STEP FOURTEEN - PRAYER WITHOUT CEASING

Maintain an attitude of prayer during the day. When you are in contact with non-Christians, pray for an opportunity to witness. Monitor your attitude and what you say or do so the Holy Spirit can use you to present a witness and draw others to Christ. When you know you are going to meet someone who is lost, pray for the filling of the Spirit and that the Spirit will show you what you should do and say to that lost person.

Transfer your practice prayer lists to the prayer lists in your prayer workbook. These prayer lists will help you organize your prayer life for years to come. Set aside a time each day to pray through your intercessory prayer lists.

For Group Discussions

1. Open with a time of prayer.

2. Review what God is doing in each person's prayer life. Pray for those who are struggling.

3. Review steps 6-10 of Global Intercessory Prayer. Discuss various types of prayer requests in each category. Make sure that each student has set up their prayer notebook correctly.

4. Discuss steps 11-14 of Global Intercessory Prayer.

5. Divide the class into groups of two. Spend the remaining time in prayer.

ASSIGNMENT: Transfer your practice prayer lists to your DAILY prayer list. Add prayer items as you feel led. Read Chapter Five by the next class meeting.

Chapter Five
Commitment

Preparation

Prepare yourself for this session with prayer. Give praise to God, confess your sins before God, and pray for the power of the Holy Spirit to work through your life. Prepare yourself to be sensitive to the leadership of the Holy Spirit for revelation, instruction, and direction.

Have a black ink pen ready to sign the commitment certificate.

Introduction

We will be looking at three different spiritual principles that may not have an apparent connection. In the end, we will draw some conclusions as we relate these different spiritual principles together that call us to prayer.

A Call to Prayer

Principle #1: God has chosen to limit the advancement of Christ's Kingdom on earth to the physical and spiritual (prayer) activities of men.

The primary concern of our study is God's limitation of His work to the prayers of men.

First of all, we have evidence that God has chosen to limit Himself to our prayers because He still commands us to make requests of Him through prayer (John 15:16 *"You did not choose Me, but I chose you, and appointed you, that you should go and bear fruit, and that your fruit should remain, that whatever you ask of the Father in My name, He may give to you."*). God is sovereign. He has chosen us. He has a design for our lives. Yet He still commands us to make requests of Him through prayer. Throughout the Old and New Testaments we are told to pray to God. God has chosen not to just send us out to bear fruit, but to send us out to bear fruit with the support of our prayers.

We have further evidence that God has chosen to limit Himself to our prayers because many of God's promises are dependent upon our prayers.

- Jeremiah 33:3 - *"Call to Me, and I will answer you, and I will tell you great and mighty things, which you do not know."* God will do things beyond what we can comprehend IF we will call upon Him through prayer.

- James 1:5 - *"But if any of you lacks wisdom, let him ask of God, who gives to all men generously and without reproach, and it will be given to him."* If we lack wisdom, it is ours IF we will just ask Him for it. This is a wonderful promise, but it is dependent upon prayer. We must ask for it.

- 2 Chronicles 7:14-15 - *"And My people who are called by My name humble themselves and pray, and seek My face and turn from their wicked ways, then I will hear from heaven, will forgive their sin, and will heal their land. Now My eyes shall be open and My ears attentive to the prayer offered in this place."* IF we will humble ourselves and pray, THEN He will heal our land and hear our prayers. Here again, God wants to work in our midst, but we must first ask Him to work through our prayers.

We have further evidence that God has chosen to limit Himself to our prayers because the great works of God are preceded by the prayers of men.

- The coming of the Holy Spirit was preceded by the prayers in the upper room. Acts 1:12-14 *"Then they returned to Jerusalem from the mount called Olivet, which is near Jerusalem, a Sabbath day's journey away. And when they had entered, they went up to the upper room, where they were staying; that is, Peter and John and James and Andrew, Philip and Thomas, Bartholomew and Matthew, James the son of Alphaeus, and Simon the Zealot, and Judas the son of James. These all with one mind were continually devoting themselves to prayer, along with the women, and Mary the mother of Jesus, and with His brothers."*

Following those prayers, God moved in a mighty and dramatic way as described in Acts 2:1-4: *"And when the day of Pentecost had come, they were all together in one place. And suddenly there came from heaven a noise like a violent, rushing wind, and it filled the whole house where they were sitting. And there appeared to them tongues as of fire distributing themselves, and they rested on each one of them. And they were all filled with the Holy Spirit and began to speak with other tongues, as the Spirit was giving them utterance."*

Even in a moment of time as important and historic as Pentecost, scripture goes to great lengths to describe how God began His work by moving men to prayer, and then responding to those prayers.

● God worked a great miracle in response to Hezekiah's prayer when the Israelites were in an impossible situation.

2 Kings 19:15-20 *"And Hezekiah prayed before the Lord and said, 'O Lord, the God of Israel, who art enthroned above the cherubim, Thou art the God, Thou alone, of all the kingdoms of the earth. Thou hast made heaven and earth. Incline Thine ear, O Lord, and hear; open Thine eyes, O Lord, and see; and listen to the words of Sennacherib, which he has sent to reproach the living God. Truly, O Lord, the kings of Assyria have devastated the nations and their lands and have cast their gods into the fire, for they were not gods but the work of men's hands, wood and stone. So they have destroyed them. And now, O Lord our God, I pray, deliver us from his hand that all the kingdoms of the earth may know that Thou alone, O Lord, art God.' Then Isaiah the son of Amoz sent to Hezekiah saying, 'Thus says the Lord, the God of Israel, "Because you have prayed to Me about Sennacherib king of Assyria, I have heard you."'"*

Notice that God responded *Because* Hezekiah prayed. And what a response it was! In 2 Kings 19:32-35 we read: *"Therefore thus says the Lord concerning the king of Assyria, 'He shall not come to this city or shoot an arrow there; neither shall he come before it with a shield, nor throw up a mound against it. By the way that he came, by the same he shall return, and he shall not come to this city,' declares the Lord. 'For I will defend this city to save it for My own sake and for My servant David's sake.' Then it happened that night that the angel of the Lord went out, and struck 185,000 in the camp of the Assyrians; and when men rose early in the morning, behold, all of them were dead."*

• Even the calling out of laborers is dependent upon our prayers. In Matthew 9:37-38 we read: *"Then He said to His disciples, 'The harvest is plentiful, but the workers are few. Therefore beseech the Lord of the harvest to send out workers into His harvest.'"* If God had not placed some sort of limitation upon Himself in relationship to our prayers, this passage would be very hard to understand. Jesus is the Lord of the Harvest, yet He is telling us to pray to Him to send out laborers. It is clear that more laborers will be sent out if we pray for them than if we do not pray for them.

Finally, we know that God has chosen to limit Himself to our prayers because when we do not know what to pray for, God Himself will pray through us. It is difficult to understand why the Holy Spirit would intercede for us through prayer unless God has chosen to limit Himself to prayer.

Romans 8:26-27 *"And in the same way the Spirit also helps our weakness; for we do not know how to pray as we should, but the Spirit Himself intercedes for us with groanings too deep for words; and He who searches the hearts knows what the mind of the Spirit is, because He intercedes for the saints according to the will of God."*

Prayer is so vital to God's work in our lives that the Spirit Himself will pray through us when we do not know what to pray in order for God's will to be accomplished in our lives.

One note of caution. When we talk about God limiting Himself, we must remember that the only limitations God has are those He has placed upon Himself, or things which are contrary to His nature. Now let's look at the second spiritual principle.

Principle #2: The Bible teaches us to pray for the second coming.

Scripture teaches us to pray for the second coming of Christ. In the Lord's prayer, Jesus taught us to pray, *Thy kingdom come.* Since this is the prayer Christ gave to us for our instruction in the 20th century as well as for the disciples, Jesus meant not only for the disciples to pray for the ushering in of the kingdom at the resurrection, but also the consummation (completion or fulfillment) of the kingdom at the second coming. Jesus knew His model prayer would be the only model He would give to us in His Holy Scripture. Then surely He intended for us to pray *Thy kingdom come* even today.

The disciples understood that they were to pray *Thy kingdom come* following the resurrection. Paul, John, and Peter all prayed for the second coming.

> • We find that Paul prayed for the second coming when he prayed *maranatha*, which means *"O, our Lord come."* (1 Cor 16:22).

> • Peter taught us that *"the end of all things is at hand, therefore be of sound judgement and sober spirit for the purpose of prayer."* (1 Peter 4:7).

> • In the Revelation of John, we also find a prayer for Christ's return. The second to last verse of the Bible is a prayer for the second coming of Christ (*"Come, Lord Jesus."* Rev 22:20b).

Now let's look at the third spiritual principle.

Principle #3: The end of the age is at hand.

First of all, we should **always** live in expectation of the second coming. Matthew 24:42-44 *"Therefore be on the alert, for you do not know which day your Lord is coming. But be sure of this, that if the head of the house had known at what time of the night the thief was coming, he would have been on the alert and would not have allowed his house to be broken into. For this reason you be ready too; for the Son of Man is coming at an hour when you do not think He will."* We should live out our lives in readiness of the imminent return of Christ.

Secondly, I believe the end of the age is at hand because global evangelization is within reach (Matthew 24:14 *"And this gospel of the kingdom shall be preached in the whole world for a witness to all the nations, and then the end shall come."*). Hundreds of mission agencies have set goals to fulfill this prophecy. It is within reach for the first time in history. When it is completed, Christ will then return.

Thirdly, I believe the end of the age is at hand because the nation of Israel has been restored. The prophecies regarding the endtime assume that Israel is a nation. Thus, only since the middle of this century has the second coming been possible.

Now let's bring these three spiritual principles together into a conclusion.

Concluding Principle: IF God has chosen to limit Himself to our prayers, and the Bible teaches us to pray for the second coming, and the end of the age is at hand, THEN God is surely calling out His people to pray.

The issue is not whether or not there will be a second coming. He will come whether we, as individuals, pray or not. He has already called people to prayer throughout the world. People have been praying since the early church. **The issue is whether we will become a part of His will, through our prayers, for all the things associated with the end of the age and the second coming of Christ.** Do you want to play a part in Christ's return?

The Bible says God will pour out a Spirit of supplication at the end of the age. (Zachariah 12:10 "*And I will pour out on the house of David and on the inhabitants of Jerusalem, the Spirit of grace and of supplication, so that they will look on Me whom they have pierced; and they will mourn for Him, as one mourns for an only son, and they will weep bitterly over Him, like the bitter weeping over a first-born.*") This Old Testament prophecy speaks specifically of a Spirit of grace and supplication (prayer) being poured out on the House of David and Jerusalem at the end of the age. The purpose of this supplication is to draw the children of Israel to Christ. In having been grafted into the vine as the children of God, we too must be encouraged that God says He will call His people to prayer to accomplish His purpose in the endtime. Surely He is calling us, His children in Christ, to pray as well.

In the countries where His spirit is moving in mighty ways (such as Korea), He has called them to prayer and they have responded. All night prayer meetings consisting of entire congregations are common. Retreats to prayer mountains for seasons of prayer and fasting are the norm. Many Koreans pray for the second coming of Christ.

While I was in Korea in 1981, we visited Prayer Mountain of Paul Cho Younggi's church. In one of the prayer caves, there was heard the wailing and crying of a Korean woman. What tragedy could have struck this woman to cause such anguish? It wasn't a personal tragedy, but a national tragedy. She was praying for God to awaken the sleeping giant, America, to the task of global evangelization. With all of her wealth and resources, what an impact America could have upon global evangelization if she could only be mobilized. What an important lesson this woman taught us. It is only through concentrated and persistent prayer that the nations will be drawn to prayer and the Great Commission.

If you belong to Him and these principles are true, then God is calling you to prayer. 1 Peter 4:7 *"The end of all things is at hand; therefore, be of sound judgment and sober spirit for the purpose of prayer."* Now is the most exciting time to have lived on earth. Christ's first coming was in humility and poverty. His second will be in glory and power. Are you willing to commit yourself to be a part of it?

Time of Commitment

Are you willing to become a Global Prayer Warrior? Such a commitment may be difficult for you, but if you are not willing to make a bold stand for prayer, it is unlikely you will be a lasting prayer intercessor. Our churches are full of people who at one time or another have desired, yet failed to improve their prayer lives. Read aloud the Prayer Intercessor Commitment Certificate on the following page. I urge you to prayerfully sign the certificate and ask someone else to sign it as a witness of your commitment. This may be a spouse, church leader, friend, or pastor. Place the certificate where you can see it during your regular prayer time. The beginning of your prayer lists is a good place. If you are not ready to sign it, continue praying about the matter.

Spend some time in prayer right now and make a commitment to Christ as a global prayer intercessor.

Prayer Intercessor

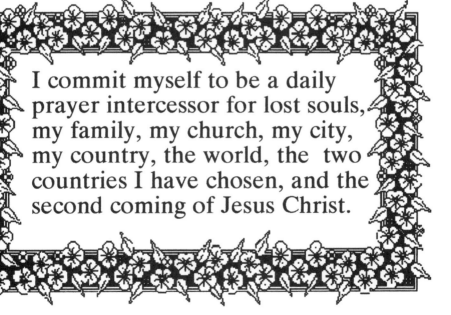

I commit myself to be a daily prayer intercessor for lost souls, my family, my church, my city, my country, the world, the two countries I have chosen, and the second coming of Jesus Christ.

_____   _____
Your Signature   Witness

Getting Started

You can prove to yourself that you can spend much more time in prayer than you imagined possible. Prayerfully set a goal from 20 minutes to one hour a day to spend in prayer over the next two months. You may be shocked at the amount of time you can spend in prayer. Many find that they never miss the time. In fact, many people are so blessed through this exercise that they maintain and even increase their prayer time after the two months are completed.

In order to keep yourself accountable, use the prayer diary on the following page to record your time in prayer each day. Begin each day with your spiritual preparation for the day. Use the checklist at the beginning of your prayer lists to guide you until you know it by memory. Then set aside a special time each day to pray through your intercessory prayer lists and *Operation World*. Spend special time in prayer as you drive your car, take a walk, or go jogging. Include prayer time with your spouse, family, or church (only the actual time in prayer). At the end of each day, write down your best estimate of the time you spent in prayer for that day. Don't keep a stop watch on your prayer time. It will only distract you. Just give it your best estimate.

At the end of your two month commitment, retake the Prayer Analysis on page 13. Spend some extended time in prayer and meditation, and talk to God about what He has been doing in your prayer life, and what He wants you to do as a prayer warrior. Seek His leadership and commit yourself to do what He leads you to do.

Prayerfully set a goal for your average time in total daily prayer over the next two months (this includes your early morning prayer time, family prayer time, your prayer lists, corporate prayer, and intermittent prayer during the day).

My goal is _____ minutes per day.

Prayer Diary

Starting date:

_____

Week One

Sunday _____

Monday _____

Tuesday _____

Wed'day _____

Thursday _____

Friday _____

Saturday _____

Week Two

Sunday _____

Monday _____

Tuesday _____

Wed'day _____

Thursday _____

Friday _____

Saturday _____

Week Three

Sunday _____

Monday _____

Tuesday _____

Wed'day _____

Thursday _____

Friday _____

Saturday _____

Week Four

Sunday _____

Monday _____

Tuesday _____

Wed'day _____

Thursday _____

Friday _____

Saturday _____

Week Five

Sunday _____

Monday _____

Tuesday _____

Wed'day _____

Thursday _____

Friday _____

Saturday _____

Week Six

Sunday _____

Monday _____

Tuesday _____

Wed'day _____

Thursday _____

Friday _____

Saturday _____

Week Seven

Sunday _____

Monday _____

Tuesday _____

Wed'day _____

Thursday _____

Friday _____

Saturday _____

Week Eight

Sunday _____

Monday _____

Tuesday _____

Wed'day _____

Thursday _____

Friday _____

Saturday _____

Week Nine

Sunday _____

Monday _____

Tuesday _____

Wed'day _____

Thursday _____

Friday _____

Saturday _____

Ending Date :

_____

Average time per

day: _____

For Group Discussions

1. Open with a time of prayer.

2. Review the three principles discussed in this chapter.

3. Review the conclusion. Enter into a time of prayer of commitment to become Global Prayer Intercessors. Sign the prayer certificates (This is a personal decision and should not be a course requirement). You may want to provide an opportunity for students to bring their certificates to the teacher in order to be signed.

4. Discuss the implications of your commitments both as individuals and for your church. Ask each student to begin keeping their prayer diary.

5. Close with group prayer.

ASSIGNMENT: Read Chapter Six by the next class meeting. Use your prayer lists and keep up with your Prayer Diary each day.

Chapter Six
Power Builders & Drainers 1 - 6

Introduction

There are specific areas related to your prayer life that will tend to build a powerful prayer life, or to drain the power from your prayer life. As you understand these areas, it enables you to concentrate on your points of weakness and build a more powerful prayer life. Many of us think that the amount of time we spend in prayer is the key to a powerful prayer life. Although powerful prayer warriors usually spend a considerable amount of time in prayer, it is not just the time that builds the power behind those prayers.

Each of the power builders and drainers are presented as a single continuum or scale. For instance, faith and doubting are two sides of the same coin. On this continuum, all of us fall on a certain point between the two extremes, while none of us will lie at either end. Determining where you fall on this continuum is a very subjective measurement. But if you prayerfully consider where you are on this continuum, it will help you to evaluate your current prayer life. Through this evaluation, you can discover areas where you need to grow in order to strengthen your prayer life.

The continuums are not in order of priority. They are all important. Nor should the length of the material on any continuum be construed as a matter of importance. There is additional material on fasting only because this area has been neglected for several decades and requires further explanation.

Here's what the continuum looks like. As you study this lesson, you will use these continuums to evaluate your prayer power.

Faith   versus   Doubting

|————————————————————|————————————————————————|

Preparation

Prepare yourself for this session with prayer. Give praise to God, confess your sins before God, and pray for the power of the Holy Spirit to work through your life. Prepare yourself to be sensitive to the leadership of the Holy Spirit for revelation, instruction, and direction.

Continuum One: Righteousness

Righteousness   versus   Sin

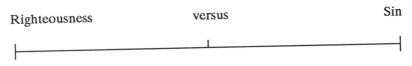

Read the following verses.

> James 5:16-18 *"Therefore, confess your sins to one another, and pray for one another, so that you may be healed. The effective prayer of a righteous man can accomplish much. Elijah was a man with a nature like ours, and he prayed earnestly that it might not rain; and it did not rain on the earth for three years and six months. And he prayed again, and the sky poured rain, and the earth produced its fruit."*

In the space provided, write your interpretation of the meaning of these verses in light of the continuum of righteousness versus sin. Does righteousness make a difference for a powerful prayer life?

(NOTE: Please do not read the commentary in the brackets until you have completed each exercise. If you can't resist, cover the commentary with a sheet of paper. Don't be concerned with right and wrong answers, that is not the purpose of this exercise. The bracketed commentary which follows your response focuses on the emphasis of this passage as it relates to this study. That emphasis may not be the only valid teaching that can be gleaned from these verses

_____

_____

_____

_____

_____

_____

[Commentary: Note that righteous living provides much power for the individual who is praying. Our power in prayer will never exceed the righteousness of our lives. We are also told that average people like us can have powerful prayer lives.]

Read the following verses.

> James 4:1-4 *What is the source of quarrels and conflicts among you? Is not the source your pleasures that wage war in your members? You lust and do not have; so you commit murder. And you are envious and cannot obtain; so you fight and quarrel. You do not have because you do not ask. You ask and do not receive, because you ask with wrong motives, so that you may spend it on your pleasures. You adulteresses, do you not know that friendship with the world is hostility toward God? Therefore whoever wishes to be a friend of the world makes himself an enemy of God.*

In the space provided, write your interpretation of the meaning of this verse in light of the continuum of righteousness versus sin. (Please do not read the information in the brackets until you have completed each exercise. If you can't resist, cover the commentary with a sheet of paper.)

_____

_____

_____

_____

_____

_____

[Commentary: This passage indicates that our prayers are not
answered because of sin in our lives. More specifically, they are not
answered because we are seeking pleasure in our own lives rather
than seeking God's will. How many of us are too comfortable in the
world with our nice homes, jobs, families, pleasures, etc. to place
God's will as the top priority? Righteous living is one of the most
important power builders of one's prayer life.]

Read the following verse.

> 1 Peter 3:12 *"For the eyes of the Lord are upon the righteous, And
> His ears attend to their prayer, But the face of the Lord is against
> those who do evil."*

In the space provided, write your interpretation of the meaning of
this verse in light of the continuum of righteousness versus sin. Does
the Lord hear those who practice evil?

_____

_____

_____

_____

_____

Read the following verse.

Isaiah 1:15 *"So when you spread out your hands in prayer, I will hide My eyes from you, Yes, even though you multiply prayers, I will not listen. Your hands are covered with blood."*

In the space provided, answer the following question. Based upon this passage, is it possible to pray to God and not be heard? If so, why?

_____

_____

_____

_____

_____

[Commentary: Not only is it possible not to be heard, we can even multiply our prayers and still not be heard if we allow unconfessed sin to build up in our lives.]

Personal Evaluation

Mark an X on the continuum at the place where you believe you presently are in your own prayer life. Mark it to the far left if your life is completely righteous. Mark it to the far right if your life is filled with conscious sin. Your mark will be somewhere between the two extremes, but do not mark your X exactly in the middle. You must lean one way or the other.

Righteousness   versus   Sin

|————————————————|————————————————|

Continuum Two: Confession

Confessed sin   versus   Unconfessed sin

├─────────────────────────┴─────────────────────────┤

This continuum differs from the first in that the focus is not on righteous living, but whether or not we regularly confess our sins and receive God's forgiveness.

Read Psalm 66:18 and Isaiah 59:2.

> Psalm 66:18 *"If I regard wickedness in my heart, The Lord will not hear."*

> Isaiah 59:1-2 *"Behold, the Lord's hand is not so short That it cannot save; Neither is His ear so dull That it cannot hear. But your iniquities have made a separation between you and your God, And your sins have hidden His face from you, so that He does not hear."*

In the space provided, write your interpretation of the meaning of these verses in light of the continuum of confessed sin versus unconfessed sin.

_____

_____

_____

_____

_____

[Commentary: It should be clear that unconfessed sin clogs up our communication channel with God. Not only are our prayers unanswered with unconfessed sin in our lives, our prayers may not even be heard.]

Read 1 John 1:6-9.

If we say that we have fellowship with Him and yet walk in the darkness, we lie and do not practice the truth; but if we walk in the light as He Himself is in the light, we have fellowship with one another, and the blood of Jesus His Son cleanses us from all sin. If we say that we have no sin, we are deceiving ourselves, and the truth is not in us. If we confess our sins, He is faithful and righteous to forgive us our sins and to cleanse us from all unrighteousness.

In the space provided, write your interpretation of the meaning of these verses in light of the continuum of confessed sin versus unconfessed sin.

_____

_____

_____

_____

_____

_____

_____

[Commentary: You cannot fellowship with Christ and walk in the darkness. Part of fellowshipping with Christ is confessing our sins to Him. If we confess our sins through prayer, Jesus will forgive us, cleanse us, and fellowship with us.]

Personal Evaluation

Place an X on the continuum that represents where you believe you presently are in your own prayer life: whether you pray with your sins confessed or left unconfessed.

Confessed sin   versus   Unconfessed sin

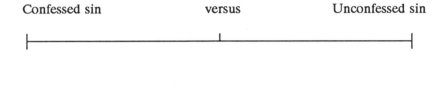

Continuum Three: Faith

Faith   versus   Doubting

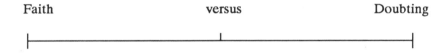

Read Matthew 17:19-20.

> *"Then the disciples came to Jesus privately and said, 'Why could we not cast it out?' And He said to them, 'Because of the littleness of your faith; for truly I say to you, if you have faith as a mustard seed, you shall say to this mountain, "Move from here to there," and it shall move; and nothing shall be impossible to you.'"*

The disciples routinely cast out evil spirits during their ministry. They were obviously surprised when they confronted an evil spirit that was too powerful for them to cast out. Jesus indicated that in spite of their failure, the spiritual power available to them was beyond their imagination, if only they had faith. What a demonstration of power to be able to literally move mountains. Prayer with faith has no limits. The more we doubt, the less power we have in prayer.

Read James 1:6-7.

"But let him ask in faith without any doubting, for the one who doubts is like the surf of the sea driven and tossed by the wind. For let not that man expect that he will receive anything from the Lord."

In the space provided, write your interpretation of the meaning of these verses in light of the continuum of faith.

_____

_____

_____

_____

_____

_____

Read Matthew 21:18-22

Now in the morning, when He returned to the city, He became hungry. And seeing a lone fig tree by the road, He came to it, and found nothing on it except leaves only; and He said to it, "No longer shall there ever be any fruit from you." And at once the fig tree withered. And seeing this, the disciples marveled, saying, "How did the fig tree wither at once?" And Jesus answered and said to them, "Truly I say to you, if you have faith, and do not doubt, you shall not only do what was done to the fig tree, but even if you say to this mountain, 'Be taken up and cast into the sea,' it shall happen. And all things you ask in prayer, believing, you shall receive."

This testimony from Christ is hard for most of us to imagine as a reality in our own lives, but the teaching is clear: prayer with faith is extremely powerful. How can we increase our faith in prayer? One way is to ask for guidance from the Spirit to show us what to pray for. If you are confident that your prayer was sourced in God and it is His will for it to be answered, then you can pray with mountain moving faith. As we begin to pray according to His will, and see those prayers answered, our confidence and faith will grow. We can dare to pray for the impossible, and see the hand of God at work as never before. But such growth in our prayer life takes time and patience. As an eight year old, one can not become a mature adult by just willing it so. Neither can you decide to become the kind of prayer warrior that can move mountains by just deciding you want to do it. It takes spiritual growth, over time, as we allow the Holy Spirit to take complete control of our life. Then the Holy Spirit molds us and shapes us through growth experiences and trials in order to conform us to the image of Christ.

Note: We cannot pray with that kind of faith for selfishly motivated prayers. Nor can we pray someone into salvation against their will.

Personal Evaluation

Place an X on the continuum that represents where you believe you presently are in your own prayer life: whether you are full of faith or doubts.

Faith   versus   Doubting

├─────────────────────────────┴──────────────────────┤

Continuum Four:
The Source

Sourced from God   versus   Sourced from self

|—————————————————|—————————————————|

This is a very difficult concept to explain. In my spiritual pilgrimage, I fought against this truth for many years because to experience it, it means that you must give over the control of your life completely to God. While I was willing to leave my home and serve God on the mission field, I always wanted to have some sense of control over my life. I wanted to have control over some of the more personal and intimate areas of my life including my prayer life. Otherwise, I argued, I was nothing more than a robot.

My real problem was that I didn't trust God. I didn't trust Him to look out for my best interests, and do the things that would bring me the greatest pleasure in life. I praise God that this barrier has now been crossed, and for the first time in my life I began to experience real joy, peace, and power in prayer.

One way to understand this concept is from an illustration of warfare. In the recent Persian Gulf War, the command and control ability of the Iraqi forces were cut. There was no communication between the central commanders and field commanders. On the battlefield, everyone was doing what they thought was best from their limited perspective. Many lives were lost, and the Iraqi armies suffered one of the most lopsided defeats in modern warfare. The allied forces, however, had control of every soldier. The commanders plotted a course to victory, and completed their plan. What was best for the whole allied force, was also the best interest of each individual. The casualties were unbelievably low; the war was over in a few days; and the soldiers returned safely home to their families.

Jesus Christ is the supreme commander of God's army in the battle to rescue a lost world from the Kingdom of Darkness. He sees the total picture, and only He knows the complete battle plan. If we will submit to His direction and seek to know His will, then He will communicate with us through our prayer life. That's what prayer is: communication with God. And when we are following His battle plan, it not only serves the best interests of God, but for each of us as well.

Prayer sourced in Christ is an outgrowth of our intimate relationship with Him and seeks His will for our lives. These prayers will certainly be answered. Prayers sourced in self are either from the flesh or an outgrowth of our personal duty as Christians to pray. If they are sourced in the flesh, then we are praying for our own selfish motives. If sourced in duty, then we are praying because we are supposed to pray (the law) rather than through our relationship with Christ (faith). If you are praying merely out of duty, then your prayer life is a burden rather than a joy.

Read the following verse.

> Galatians 4:6 "*And because you are sons, <u>God has sent forth</u> the Spirit of His Son into our hearts, crying, 'Abba! Father!'*"

In the space provided, write your interpretation of the meaning of this verse in light of the continuum of our prayer source. What is this verse describing?

_____

_____

_____

_____

_____

[Commentary: God is sourcing our prayers by sending the Spirit into our hearts, who in turn is praying back to the Father in a personal and intimate way.]

Read the following verses.

Romans 8:26-27 *"And in the same way the Spirit also helps our weakness; for we do not know how to pray as we should, but the Spirit Himself intercedes for us with groanings too deep for words; and He who searches the hearts knows what the mind of the Spirit is, because He intercedes for the saints according to the will of God."*

In the space provided, write your interpretation of the meaning of these verses in light of the continuum of our prayer source.

_____

_____

_____

_____

_____

_____

[Commentary: Prayer is so important to God's working in our lives, that if we do not know how to pray for ourselves, the Spirit of God will pray through us on our behalf.]

Read the following verse.

Ephesians 6:18 *"With all prayer and petition pray at all times in the Spirit, and with this in view, be on the alert with all perseverance and petition for all the saints."*

In the space provided, write your interpretation of the meaning of this verse **in light of the continuum of our prayer source.**

_____

_____

_____

_____

_____

[Commentary: Praying *in the Spirit* includes placing the Spirit in control of our prayer lives.]

If you will allow the Holy Spirit to source prayers through your life, the Holy Spirit will begin to bring people and events to your mind in order to draw you to prayer. This is one of the first signs that may indicate you are becoming a prayer warrior. This doesn't mean you will hear voices or feel some great emotion, but if you are alert in your prayers, when a friend or situation comes to your mind, just whisper a prayer for that person or event. If you are faithful in praying in this way, the Spirit himself will bring prayer needs to your mind, knowing that you will be faithful in prayer.

I can give many illustrations of this truth. One night, my wife and I were watching the news. They were telling of a typhoon headed toward the Philippines. My wife, Linda, turned to me immediately and said, "Bob and Jan Nash!" Bob and Jan are missionary friends of ours serving in the Philippines. Linda was impressed that we should pray for them. While we know many missionaries in the Philippines, the Spirit was impressing on us to pray for this couple. So we did.

Later we learned that Bob and Jan had been traveling on an isolated mountain road when we were praying for them. At that time, an earthquake struck. Just in front of them, the road collapsed and slid down the mountain. It was a narrow escape from a certain death. Then the road collapsed behind them too. There they stood, trapped on the only piece of the road that remained on a treacherous mountain side. A party of students noticed they were missing and mounted a search party to hike through the jungle to find them. Several days later, they were rescued. As this potential catastrophe began, the Holy Spirit reached across the globe and touched the heart of prayer warriors to pray for the Nashes. Those Spirit sourced prayers were then answered.

Personal Evaluation

Place an X on your continuum that represents where you believe you presently are in your own prayer life: whether it is sourced in Christ or self. If fully sourced from God, it would be to the far left; if fully sourced in self, it would be to the far right.

Sourced from God   versus   Sourced from self

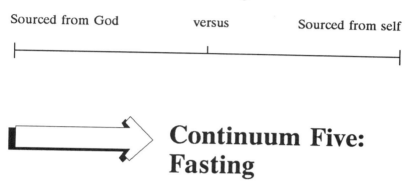

Continuum Five: Fasting

Fasting   versus   Undisciplined Lifestyle

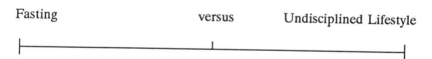

In the beginning of Chapter 58, Isaiah is describing God's displeasure with the things associated with the practice of fasting among the Israelites at that time. The people were fasting as they had been taught to do, but they were doing it with the wrong motives and for the wrong reasons. God did not honor or respond to those fasts. This chapter does not teach that God didn't want people to fast any more. Fasting obviously continued throughout the Old and New Testament times. Jesus fasted and told us to do the same. In this passage, God is telling us the kinds of things that should be associated with our fasting, and what His response will be to those fasts.

Isaiah 58:6-11: *"Is this not the fast which I choose, To loosen the bonds of wickedness, To undo the bands of the yoke, And to let the oppressed go free, And break every yoke? Is it not to divide your bread with the hungry, And bring the homeless poor into the house; When you see the naked, to cover him; And not to hide yourself from your own flesh? Then your light will break out like the dawn, And your recovery will speedily spring forth; And your righteousness will go before you; The glory of the Lord will be your rear guard. Then you will call, and the Lord will answer; You will cry, and He will say, 'Here I am.' If you remove the yoke from your midst, The pointing of the finger, and speaking wickedness, And if you give yourself to the hungry, And satisfy the desire of the afflicted, Then your light will rise in darkness, And your gloom will become like midday. And the Lord will continually guide you, And satisfy your desire in scorched places, And give strength to your bones; And you will be like a watered garden, And like a spring of water whose waters do not fail."*

What is Fasting?

Fasting is focusing away from the things of this world, in order to commune with God. The things of this world focus on our basic biological need for sustenance. Communion with God takes place through prayer, meditation, and the reading of God's Word.

Why should we Fast?

1. Jesus told us we would fast after His ascension.

> Matthew 9:14-15 *"Then the disciples of John came to Him, saying, 'Why do we and the Pharisees fast, but Your disciples do not fast?' And Jesus said to them, 'The attendants of the bridegroom cannot mourn as long as the bridegroom is with them, can they? But the days will come when the bridegroom is taken away from them, and then they will fast.'"*

This includes us, now! The bridegroom has been taken away. Jesus is calling us to fast.

2. God listens to our fast.

> Ezra 8:21-23 *"Then I proclaimed a fast there at the river of Ahava, that we might humble ourselves before our God to seek from Him a*

safe journey for us, our little ones, and all our possessions. For I was ashamed to request from the king troops and horsemen to protect us from the enemy on the way, because we had said to the king, 'The hand of our God is favorably disposed to all those who seek Him, but His power and His anger are against all those who forsake Him. So we fasted and sought our God concerning this matter, and He listened to our entreaty.'"

Fasting is an exclamation point to God. It is a statement of our sincerity beyond mere words. It is a demonstration of faithfulness.

3. There is power in fasting.

Matthew 17:19-21: *"Then the disciples came to Jesus privately and said, 'Why could we not cast it out?' And He said to them, 'Because of the littleness of your faith; for truly I say to you, if you have faith as a mustard seed, you shall say to this mountain, "move from here to there," and it shall move and nothing shall be impossible to you. But this kind does not go out except by prayer and fasting.'"*

> Note: Verse 21 is not found in some manuscripts and thus some doubt that Jesus said it. But many manuscripts do contain this verse, including the Coptic manuscript from the 6th century. There are only two choices for the interpretation of this textual problem: either Jesus said it, or the early church (which turned the world upside down with its power) could not understand this verse unless prayer and fasting had been the intention. Either way, it is a testimony to the power of prayer and fasting. Personally, I believe Jesus said it.

The disciples were accustomed to claiming their Christ given authority over the demons. But now they had encountered a demon whose power was too great for them to cast out. Jesus, of course, had no problem since His power has no equal. But this verse indicates that the disciples could claim additional power beyond what they had previously known through prayer and fasting.

4. God will reward our fasts.

Matthew 6:16-18 *"And whenever you fast, do not put on a gloomy face as the hypocrites do, for they neglect their appearance in order to be seen fasting by men. Truly I say to you, they have their reward in full. But you, when you fast, anoint your head, and wash your face so that you may not be seen fasting by men, but by your Father who is in secret; and your Father who sees in secret will repay you."*

God will repay us for our fasts. How does he repay us? Write your answer in the space provided.

_____

_____

_____

_____

[Commentary: He repays us in many ways, but certainly one of them is through answered prayer.]

What is the Purpose of Fasting?

1. To seek God's direction (His will) whether it be personal or corporate.

In 2 Chronicles, Judah was facing certain defeat from a mighty army. Jehoshaphat didn't know what to do, so he proclaimed a fast and sought the Lord for an answer.

> 2 Chronicles 20: *(3) "And Jehoshaphat was afraid and turned his attention to seek the Lord; and proclaimed a fast throughout all Judah. (12) 'O our God, wilt Thou not judge them? For we are powerless before this great multitude who are coming against us; nor do we know what to do, but our eyes are on Thee.' (14) Then in the midst of the assembly the Spirit of the Lord came upon Jahaziel the son of Zechariah, the son of Benaiah, the son of Jeiel, the son of Mattaniah, the Levite of the sons of Asaph; (15) and he said, 'Listen, all Judah and the inhabitants of Jerusalem and King Jehoshaphat: thus says the Lord to you, "Do not fear or be dismayed because of this great multitude, for the battle is not yours but God's. (17) You need not fight in this battle; station yourselves, stand and see the salvation of the Lord on your behalf, O Judah and Jerusalem. Do not fear or be dismayed; tomorrow go out to face them, for the Lord is with you."' (22) And when they began singing and praising, the Lord set ambushes against the sons of Ammon, Moab, and Mount Seir, who had come against Judah; so they were routed. (24) When Judah came*

to the lookout of the wilderness, they looked toward the multitude; and behold, they were corpses lying on the ground, and no one had escaped."

Whenever I make a major decision, I want the assurance that it is God's will for my life. In order to ensure that I am in His will, I enter into a season (time) of prayer and fasting. He has always honored those fasts and given me a clear direction that was certainly His will. A church should also seek the Lord's will for major decisions through corporate prayer and fasting. Does your church enter into a season of prayer and fasting when it selects a pastor, elders, or deacons?

Acts 13:2 *"And while they were ministering to the Lord and fasting, the Holy Spirit said, 'Set apart for Me Barnabas and Saul for the work to which I have called them.'"*

Acts 14:23 *"And when they had appointed elders for them in every church, having prayed with fasting, they commended them to the Lord in whom they had believed."*

There are also times when we sense a distance from God. Through prayer and fasting we can draw very close to Him.

2. Fasting can produce spiritual power for engaging in spiritual warfare with the forces of darkness.

• In your personal life, fasting can provide power for intercession, healing, and deliverance from the Evil One. While serving as a missionary in Singapore, there was an area of personal sin in my life that I had tried to control for many years. But no matter how hard I tried, I could not release myself from the grip it had on my life. A fellow missionary suggested that I try a season of prayer and fasting to be delivered from this bondage. I entered into three days of prayer and fasting and found deliverance. I was freed and have remained free ever since.

• When we are confronted with someone who seems to be blinded to the truths of the Gospel, we can enter into a season of prayer and fasting for that person's salvation. We should pray against any evil or deluding spirit upon that person's life so that this person may have the freedom to fully understand the claims of Christ and have the personal freedom to accept or reject Christ without the interference of the Evil One. We cannot pray someone into salvation, but we can pray against the spiritual forces that may have kept that person from having a chance to hear the truth of the Gospel.

● The church has been given a great power against the Kingdom of Darkness in corporate prayer and fasting. Satan has blinded many evangelical churches concerning the use of the most potent weapon we have against him. No wonder so many of our churches are so weak and powerless. After hearing a sermon on fasting, the members of a home fellowship group at Nursery Road Presbyterian Church in Columbia, South Carolina decided to enter into a season of prayer and fasting for the salvation of several people they had been praying for. One man had been praying for the salvation of his father for 17 years with no breakthrough. Within one week of their fast, that group saw two people accept Christ as Lord and Savior, including the man's father.

3. Another purpose of fasting is to humble ourselves before God, repent of our sins, ask for mercy, and pray for a renewed relationship with God.

Jonah 3: 5, 10: *"Then the people of Ninevah believed in God; and they called a fast and put on sack cloth from the greatest to the least of them. (10) When God saw their deeds, that they turned from their wicked way, then God relented concerning the calamity which he had declared He would bring upon them. And He did not do it."*

Although the context here is for a nation, it is valid for the church and individuals as well. I believe it would be appropriate for a church that is spiritually dead or full of sin to call for a fast and pray for forgiveness, mercy, restoration, and renewal.

When should we fast?

1. We should fast at God's initiative. This isn't just for fasting. We should always seek God's leadership in the things we do. Something as important as fasting should be no different. We should approach God to determine if we should fast, either as an individual or corporately. Should you fast about a certain matter? Don't answer

78

flippantly. Ask God if He wants you to fast. Fasting for the sake of ritual or out of duty is not honored. If you fast regularly, make sure there is a valid purpose or reason for those fasts.

2. Missing one meal can hardly be described as a fast. In fact, if I just skip a meal, I get so hungry that I often feel sick. The feeling of hunger is generated from a shrinking stomach. After you eat breakfast, or lunch, you feel hunger when your stomach starts to shrink after the food is passed along. During the night, you feel no hunger because you are asleep while your stomach is shrinking. Many people who think they cannot fast will think nothing of missing breakfast in the morning after they have not eaten for about 12 hours. But after eating, they are famished after only a few hours.

After I was properly taught to fast, I have personally not gotten weak, sick, or felt starved. A fast is begun after an evening meal; no solid food is eaten during the following day or days; and the fast is broken either in the morning or in the evening.

3. The ending of a fast should also be at God's initiative. As your fast progresses, seek God's guidance as to when the fast should be ended. Don't let your ego take control and attempt to see how long you can fast in order to prove something to God or others. I have never fasted more than three days because I have never felt led to do so. When I feel led, I will gladly obey. We can trust God to lead us in fasting.

How does one Fast?

1. Preparation

   ● Get off caffeine several days before you begin. This includes coffee, tea, chocolate, and many soft drinks, such as colas, orange, etc. Caffeine is a powerful, addicting drug. When we stop our intake of caffeine, there are withdrawal symptoms, the most problematic being headaches. Some people have headaches when they fast and blame it on the fasting when the problem is really caffeine withdrawal.

   ● The evening meal before your fast should be small, with lots of fiber/vegetables, little fat, and no refined sugar.

● If you have any medical problems, check with your doctor before you begin a fast that extends for a day or more.

2. During the fast

● Eat no solid foods, but drink plenty of liquids. Most people drink only water, while others will include some sort of juice. Grape, apple, or tomato juices are good choices, while citric juices are not good for fasting. If you have a medical condition where maintaining a certain level of blood sugar is important, you should take some juice with your water during fasting (consult your physician). Since the body cleanses itself during a fast, pure distilled water is the best liquid for cleansing your system. Pure H_2O cleanses better than tap water which contains many minerals and pollutants that alter the cleansing properties of the water.

● Go through your regularly scheduled routine as if you were not fasting. Spend extra time during your meal times in prayer and Bible study. Spend time in prayer through the day in the midst of your routine. Set aside some quality time for prayer in the morning and during the evening. You can easily spend two to four hours in prayer and reading the Word during a day of fasting.

3. Ending the fast

● Break your fast with a small meal. Eat a nutritious meal with no fried foods or refined sugar. Refined sugar on an empty stomach can damage the lining of your stomach. Some low fat yogurt will help replenish the good bacteria in your intestinal tract if you have fasted several days.

Personal Evaluation

In a spiritual sense, the opposite of fasting can best be described as an undisciplined lifestyle. Fasting is a discipline that denies some of the basic desires and needs of our bodies for the sake of accomplishing something in the spiritual realm. When we are not willing to make personal sacrifices in order to intercede for others, and are most concerned about having personal control over our actions, then in a spiritual sense our lifestyle is uncontrolled. For further reading about fasting see: *God's Chosen Fast* by Wallis, and *Fasting Changed My Life* by Anderson.

Place an X on the continuum that represents where you believe you presently are in your own prayer life in the area of fasting.

Fasting   versus   Undisciplined Lifestyle

|————————————————————|————————————————————|

Continuum Six: Preciseness

Specific Prayers   versus   General prayers

|————————————————————|————————————————————|

Read Philippians 4:6.

"Be anxious for nothing, but in everything by prayer and supplication with thanksgiving let your requests be made known to God."

In the space provided, write your interpretation of the meaning of this verse in light of this continuum.

_____

_____

_____

[Commentary: We should let our requests be made known to God "in everything," both small matters and large. We should be anxious for nothing, for all matters should be matters of prayer.]

As you plan out each day, do you pray about what God would have you do for that day? If you have more things to do than can be done, how do you determine which things will be done and which things will be left off? Do you personally make a quick decision about your priorities, or do you pray and ask God to set your priorities for the coming day? Are there small annoying problems in your life? Have you prayed about them?

Paul says that we should pray without ceasing. This doesn't mean that we should pray all day long. It means that we should be prayerfully alert in our daily lives and ask God for direction in the daily activities of life. Too many times we think of our prayer life as that time which begins with "Dear Heavenly Father," and ends with "Amen." But with a lifestyle of prayer, we can commune with God with our eyes open, while driving the car, while eating a meal, while working, before making any decision, before meeting a new person, or any other time so that we can know God's will for our lives in all things.

Personal Evaluation

Place an X on the continuum that represents where you believe you presently are in your own prayer life: making requests in everything or making requests for emergencies or for general matters.

Specific Prayers   versus   General prayers

|------------------------------|------------------------------|

Closing Prayer

The closing prayer for this chapter should be a time of personal examination of the different areas of power builders and drainers. Request the Holy Spirit to convict you of any areas of sin. Appeal to Jesus to change you and to teach and motivate you to pray.

For Group Discussions

You will probably need two sessions to complete this chapter.

1. Open with a time of prayer.

2. Review each continuum. Ask for testimonies from participants that reveal the truths of the different principles studied. If no one has experienced the truths as taught in Scripture, discuss the reasons why these areas have been neglected, and how we can incorporate them into our lifestyles.

3. Make sure each student has completed their personal evaluation on each continuum. Allow class members to share their personal evaluations if they desire to, but do not pressure students to do so against their will.

4. Spend at least the last 5 minutes of each session in prayer.

ASSIGNMENT: Ask class members to complete Chapter Seven by the next class.

Chapter Seven
Power Builders & Drainers 7 - 11

Preparation

Prepare yourself for this session with prayer. Give praise to God, confess your sins before God, and pray for the power of the Holy Spirit to work through your life. Prepare yourself to be sensitive to the leadership of the Holy Spirit for revelation, instruction, and direction.

 **Continuum Seven:**
Persistence

Persistence   versus   Inconsistency

Read Luke 18:1-8.

"Now He was telling them a parable to show that at all times they ought to pray and not to lose heart, saying, 'There was in a certain city a judge who did not fear God, and did not respect man. And there was a widow in that city, and she kept coming to him, saying, "Give me legal protection from my opponent." And for a while he was unwilling; but afterward he said to himself, "Even though I do not fear God nor respect man, yet because this widow bothers me, I will give her legal protection, lest by continually coming she wear me out."' And the Lord said, 'Hear what the unrighteous judge said; now shall not God bring about justice for His elect, who cry to Him day and night, and will He delay long over them? I tell you that He will bring about

justice for them speedily. However, when the Son of Man comes, will He find faith on the earth?"

In the space provided, write your interpretation of the meaning of these verses in light of this continuum.

_____

_____

_____

_____

_____

_____

Read Luke 11:5-13.

"And He said to them, 'Suppose one of you shall have a friend, and shall go to him at midnight, and say to him, "Friend, lend me three loaves; for a friend of mine has come to me from a journey, and I have nothing to set before him"; and from inside he shall answer and say, "Do not bother me; the door has already been shut and my children and I are in bed; I cannot get up and give you anything." I tell you, even though he will not get up and give him anything because he is his friend, yet because of his persistence he will get up and give him as much as he needs. And I say to you, ask, and it shall be given to you; seek, and you shall find; knock, and it shall be opened to you. For everyone who asks, receives; and he who seeks, finds; and to him who knocks, it shall be opened. Now suppose one of you fathers is asked by his son for a fish; he will not give him a snake instead of a fish, will he? Or if he is asked for an egg, he will not give him a scorpion, will he? If you then, being evil, know how to give good gifts to your children, how much more shall your heavenly Father give the Holy Spirit to those who ask Him?"

In the space provided, write your interpretation of the meaning of these verses in light of this continuum.

_____

_____

_____

_____

_____

_____

[Commentary: Both of these passages indicate that God wants us to be persistent and work hard in our praying. Jesus is telling us in these parables that God will honor such persistence. It is also implied that certain prayers will not be answered without such persistence.]

Personal Evaluation

Place an X on the continuum that represents where you believe you presently are in your own prayer life: persistent or inconsistent.

Persistence   versus   Inconsistency

├──────────────────────────────┴──────────────────────────────┤

Continuum Eight: Warrior

Warfare   versus   No belief in Satan

├─────────────────────────────────────┴──────────────────────┤

Read Ephesians 6:12 and 2 Corinthians 10: 3-5.

Ephesians 6:12 *"For our struggle is not against flesh and blood, but against the rulers, against the powers, against the world forces of this darkness, against the spiritual forces of wickedness in the heavenly places."*

2 Corinthians 10:3-5 *"For though we walk in the flesh, we do not war according to the flesh, for the weapons of our warfare are not of the flesh, but divinely powerful for the destruction of fortresses. We are destroying speculations and every lofty thing raised up against the knowledge of God, and we are taking every thought captive to the obedience of Christ."*

In the space provided, write your interpretation of the meaning of these verses in light of this continuum.

_____

_____

_____

_____

_____

[Commentary: We are really involved in a war between Satan and God. We must engage in this spiritual warfare and defeat the evil powers before we can accomplish the spiritual ends we so desire. The battle is won in the spiritual realm; thus our prayers are more important than our physical activities or programs.]

Read Matthew 6:13.

"And do not lead us into temptation, but deliver us from evil."

What are we praying for when we pray this portion of the model prayer?

_____

_____

_____

_____

_____

[Commentary: The word translated "evil" is actually the Evil One, i.e., Satan. Jesus is teaching us to pray for protection from Satan on a daily basis.]

Read 1 John 5:19.

"We know that we are of God, and the whole world lies in the power of the Evil One."

In the space provided, write your interpretation of the meaning of this verse in light of this continuum.

_____

_____

_____

_____

_____

[Commentary: Note that the whole world is in the power of the Evil One, but we are not under Satan's power and dominion because we belong to God.]

The Evil One has real power, and only through the power of God can Satan be overcome. Without the power of God, we can do nothing.

Personal Evaluation

Place an X on the continuum that represents where you believe you presently are in your own prayer life: whether or not you are daily engaged in spiritual warfare.

Warfare   versus   No belief in Satan

|———————————————————————————|————————————————————————|

Continuum Nine:
The Word

Reading the Bible   versus   Not reading

Read John 15:7.

"If you abide in Me, and My words abide in you, ask whatever you wish, and it shall be done for you."

In the space provided, write your interpretation of the meaning of this verse in light of this continuum.

_____

_____

_____

_____

_____

[Commentary: It is important to notice that answered prayer in this verse is conditional. **IF** Christ's words abide in us, **THEN** He will do anything we ask. Scripture reading is more than just learning about God; it is a very important prerequisite of communication with God and intercessory prayer.]

Read Psalms 119:169-175 several times.

Let my cry come before Thee, O Lord; Give me understanding according to Thy word. Let my supplication come before Thee; Deliver me according to Thy word. Let my lips utter praise, For Thou dost teach me Thy statutes. Let my tongue sing of Thy word, For all Thy commandments are righteousness. Let Thy hand be ready to help me, For I have chosen Thy precepts. I long for Thy salvation, O Lord, And Thy law is my delight. Let my soul live that it may praise Thee, And let Thine ordinances help me.

In the space provided, write your interpretation of the meaning of these verses as to their relationship to prayer and God's Word.

_____

_____

_____

_____

_____

Personal Evaluation

Place an X on the continuum that represents where you believe you presently are in your own prayer life: the daily reading of God's word or not reading the Bible.

Reading the Bible   versus   Not reading

├─────────────────────────┴────────────────────────┤

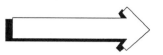

Continuum Ten:
Love

Loving relationships   versus   Dissension

Read 1 Peter 3:7.

> *"You husbands likewise, live with your wives in an understanding way,*
> *as with a weaker vessel, since she is a woman; and grant her honor as*
> *a fellow heir of the grace of life, so that your prayers may not be*
> *hindered."*

In the space provided, write your interpretation of the meaning of
this verse in light of this continuum. The last phrase is the key.

_____

_____

_____

_____

_____

_____

[Commentary: One of the areas where Satan can most easily defeat us
is in our relationship with our spouses. Notice that this passage
indicates that our prayer lives are hindered when our relationship
with our spouses is not right.]

Read 1 Peter 4:7-9.

> *"The end of all things is at hand; therefore, be of sound judgment and sober spirit for the purpose of prayer. Above all, keep fervent in your love for one another, because love covers a multitude of sins. Be hospitable to one another without complaint."*

Notice the relationship between prayer and the Second Coming of Christ. Above all, in order to accomplish this prayer, we must maintain a loving relationship with one another. This love for one another will even help overcome the problem of sin which hinders our prayer life. One of the greatest weaknesses that drains the power of our churches is dissension and wrong relationships in the fellowship.

Personal Evaluation

Place an X on the continuum that represents where you believe you presently are in your own prayer life: loving relationships with your spouse and others versus wrong attitudes such as pride, hatred, holding grudges, etc.

Loving relationships   versus   Dissension

|———————————————————⌐——————————————————|

Continuum Eleven: Forgiveness

Forgiveness   versus   Bitterness

|—————————————————|—————————————————|

Read Matthew 6:9-15.

"Pray, then, in this way:

> *'Our Father who art in heaven, Hallowed be Thy name. Thy kingdom come. Thy will be done, On earth as it is in heaven. Give us this day our daily bread. And forgive us our debts, as we also have forgiven our debtors. And do not lead us into temptation, but deliver us from evil. For Thine is the kingdom, and the power, and the glory, forever. Amen.'*

For if you forgive men for their transgressions, your heavenly Father will also forgive you. But if you do not forgive men, then your Father will not forgive your transgressions."

Following the model prayer, Jesus re-emphasizes a part of the model prayer. Why do you think Jesus added this commentary? Describe what Jesus was trying to emphasize in your own words.

_____

_____

_____

_____

Later in Mark, while talking about prayer, Jesus talks about forgiveness again. Read Mark 11:25.

"And whenever you stand praying, forgive, if you have anything against anyone; so that your Father also who is in heaven may forgive you your transgressions."

What is forgiveness? Many of us have the misconception that forgiveness means forgetting. But there is no way we can remove the memories of the past. We can suppress those memories, but there are still triggers that will bring them to our minds again. The practical side of forgiveness means that we will not make decisions in the future based upon our knowledge of what someone has done in the past. In other words, we no longer hold that person accountable to us for what they did. We release them from their moral obligation to make things right (restitution), and turn the situation over to Christ (Romans 12:19). Our bitterness and hate is turned into love and compassion. Our pain and bondage is turned into freedom and joy.

Why is forgiveness so important to our prayer lives? If we do not forgive others, then God does not forgive us. Forgiveness is part of the cleansing necessary to draw close to God in prayer. We can only walk in the Light when we forgive and are forgiven. John, who is writing to believers, says when we hate our brother, we are blinded by darkness (evil). Read 1 John 2:9 - 11.

The one who says he is in the light and yet hates his brother is in the darkness until now. The one who loves his brother abides in the light and there is no cause for stumbling in him. But the one who hates his brother is in the darkness and walks in the darkness, and does not know where he is going because the darkness has blinded his eyes.

Spend a few moments now in prayer. Prayerfully meditate upon your early years when you were growing up. Trace your life up until now and ask the Holy Spirit to reveal to you any people in your life that you have not truly forgiven. This might include parents, friends, co-workers, bosses, spouses, etc. As you pray, list the names of the people the Holy Spirit brings to your mind in the space provided.

_____

_____

_____

_____

_____

_____

The only one who gains by your refusing to forgive anyone on the list above is the Evil One. He uses your bitterness to blind you, to maintain a barrier between you and your fellowship with God, and to rob you of the power of your prayer life. The one who sinned against you is not affected by your bitterness. The real loser in a failure to forgive is yourself. **There is nothing that anyone can do to you that is worse than the consequences of unforgiveness.** If you refuse to forgive, regardless of what someone has done to you, then you are allowing Satan to control your decision in this area. By forgiving, you are making a choice to obey God and be freed from Satan's influence. Forgiveness is a choice. Forgiveness is obedience to God. Forgiveness allows us to commune with God, which brings joy and peace to our lives.

Now for each person on your list above, pray a prayer of forgiveness (i.e. Lord, I forgive ___[person's name]___ for ___[list specific memories or painful experiences of what they did that needs forgiveness]___ _____.)

Personal Evaluation

On this continuum, you will be placing two X's. Place an X on the continuum that represents where you believe you were before your prayer for forgiveness in the exercise on the previous page. Now place an X on the continuum that represents where you believe you presently are in your own prayer life: forgiveness versus bitterness.

Forgiveness   versus   Bitterness

|————————————————————————————————|

If you have been living a lifestyle of forgiveness, then the two X's are in the same place. If there was bitterness in your life which you have now been freed from through forgiveness, mark your calendar to remind you to read through this continuum again in two weeks. At that time, evaluate yourself again on the continuum. Are you satisfied with the direction you are headed? Have you noticed any changes in your life?

Closing Prayer

The closing prayer for this chapter should be a time of personal examination of the different areas of power builders and drainers. Request the Holy Spirit to convict you of any areas of sin. Appeal to Jesus to change you and to teach and motivate you to pray.

For Group Discussions

1. Open with a time of prayer.

2. Review each continuum. Ask for testimonies from participants that reveal the truths of the different principles studied. If no one has experienced the truths as taught in Scripture, discuss the reasons why these areas have been neglected, and how we can incorporate them into our lifestyles.

3. Make sure each student has completed their personal evaluation on each continuum. Allow class members to share their personal evaluations if they desire to, but do not pressure students to do so against their will.

4. Spend at least the last 5 minutes of each session in prayer.

ASSIGNMENT: Ask class members to complete Chapter Eight by the next class meeting.

Chapter Eight
Your Church

Preparation

Prepare yourself for this session with prayer. Give praise to God, confess your sins before God, and pray for the power of the Holy Spirit to work through your life. Prepare yourself to be sensitive to the leadership of the Holy Spirit for revelation, instruction, and direction.

The exercise in this chapter does not presume that your church's prayer ministry is either weak or excellent. If it is excellent, this exercise will help demonstrate to you why your church is doing what it is doing. If it is weak, then pray for your church and its leadership that their prayer lives would grow. You may want to challenge them to work through these materials. But be very careful not to aggressively confront, publicly challenge, or gossip about your church leaders and thus be used of Satan to create dissension in the body. It will be your warfare in the heavenlies (prayer), not confrontation in the physical realm, that will draw people to prayer.

Ideas for Your Church

Does your church compile prayer lists? If so, what is done with them? Do church members take these prayer lists home and pray daily for the church's needs or are they left in the pews? Determine how church prayer requests can be updated in a standard format (such as 5-1/2" x 8-1/2") to be included in individuals' prayer notebooks each week. Who will be responsible; who will do the secretarial work?

Prayer lists may be distributed in weekly prayer meetings or through your church's small groups. In cell churches, corporate prayer needs can be distributed weekly through the cell groups with space to add prayer needs of group members. These prayer lists may be distributed through the Sunday School in traditional churches.

What can the church do to provide for extensive corporate prayer power to engage in local and global warfare? Does the weekly prayer meeting (if there is one) need overhauling to become the central focus of prayer power for the work of the church? Is your prayer service just another worship service or is it an hour of power? What about Concerts of Prayer that extend for several hours for specific issues, problems, evangelistic thrusts, etc.?

When emergencies arise in the church, how can a mighty prayer army be called forth on short notice? Consider establishing prayer chains. If you already have prayer chains, are they being utilized to their full potential? If you have a prayer chain, when is the last time it was used? What do you consider a crisis big enough to call the prayer chain? Which of the following is the most important prayer need:

A. A church member is going to witness to a neighbor;

B. Aunt Martha broke her leg; or

C. A church member is having open heart surgery.

Write your answer here: _____

All are important, but nothing that happens in a person's life is more important than their eternal salvation. The answer must be "A".

Evaluate the prayer power available during the church worship services. Consider starting prayer teams to pray during services or during church visitation times. Train Christians to pray during altar calls or public invitations. Let the choir sing and the people pray.

Consider calling for days of prayer and fasting as a church. These days should have a special purpose where prayer power is necessary. How many churches call good people to join their staffs, but things don't work out because they were not God's choice for this position at this particular time. The biblical way for a church to choose leadership is through corporate prayer and fasting, but few churches follow this example.

As a church, consider becoming prayer partners with a mission field. If there is strong support for more than one partnership, include more than one, possibly with a rotating emphasis. Don't let disagreements over the choice of a foreign field be used by Satan to disrupt the body.

Your church should also be in partnership with at least one specific missionary. Encourage this missionary to send prayer requests and answers on a monthly or quarterly basis. Compile these requests in a 5 1/2" x 8 1/2" format so your prayer warriors can put them into their daily prayer lists.

You should also pray regularly for the calling out of missionaries from your church.

Provide for ongoing training in global intercessory prayer. A *Global Intercessory Prayer Course* might be taught yearly to newcomers and youth as a twelve week course; or begin a waiting list and when 10-15 people are on the waiting list, start a new course. You may also give this workbook to individuals for self-study. You can also teach this material in a workshop.

A prayer committee or other existing body should be given responsibility for implementing the prayer ministry. If no one has the responsibility, then the job will not get done. Remember that prayer, on which everything else depends, should be one of the highest priorities of your church.

Order materials from Appendix A or other sources as resources for individuals' prayer lists. These should be available in your church library.

Consider establishing a house of prayer led by godly widows who live there and have been called to a life of intercessory prayer. Study the following passage.

1 Timothy 5:1-16 *"Do not sharply rebuke an older man, but rather appeal to him as a father, to the younger men as brothers, the older women as mothers, and the younger women as sisters, in all purity. Honor widows who are widows indeed; but if any widow has children or grandchildren, let them first learn to practice piety in regard to their own family, and to make some return to their parents; for this is acceptable in the sight of God. Now she who is a widow indeed, and who has been left alone has fixed her hope on God, and continues in entreaties and prayers night and day. But she who gives herself to*

wanton pleasure is dead even while she lives. Prescribe these things as well, so that they may be above reproach. But if anyone does not provide for his own, and especially for those of his household, he has denied the faith, and is worse than an unbeliever. Let a widow be put on the list only if she is not less than sixty years old, having been the wife of one man, having a reputation for good works; and if she has brought up children, if she has shown hospitality to strangers, if she has washed the saints' feet, if she has assisted those in distress, and if she has devoted herself to every good work. But refuse to put younger widows on the list, for when they feel sensual desires in disregard of Christ, they want to get married, thus incurring condemnation, because they have set aside their previous pledge. And at the same time they also learn to be idle, as they go around from house to house; and not merely idle, but also gossips and busybodies, talking about things not proper to mention. Therefore, I want younger widows to get married, bear children, keep house, and give the enemy no occasion for reproach; for some have already turned aside to follow Satan. If any woman who is a believer has dependent widows, let her assist them, and let not the church be burdened, so that it may assist those who are widows indeed."

Notice the following points about this passage:

1. These are widows who have apparently pooled their resources and are being supported by the church.

2. There are stringent moral and spiritual requirements that would be needed for a powerful prayer intercessor.

3. They have made a pledge.

4. They are continual prayer warriors that undergird the ministry of the church.

What an exciting possibility; a house of prayer where prayer is continually offered to God; a place for any church member to go to have someone to pray with them. The possibilities are limitless.

Is it feasible to incorporate this into the life of your church? Explain why or why not.

_____

_____

_____

_____

_____

Church Evaluation

List the existing formal prayer ministries of your church. These might include prayer services, prayer chains, the role of prayer in worship services, prayer for evangelism, prayer education, prayer in small groups (cells or home fellowships), etc. Evaluate these ministries individually and as a whole in light of what has been learned in this prayer guide. Is your prayer ministry accomplishing what was intended? Is it providing the prayer power needed to accomplish the mission of the church?

Church Prayer Ministry #1

Description _____

_____

Evaluation _____

_____

_____

_____

Church Prayer Ministry #2

Description _____

_____

Evaluation _____

_____

_____

_____

Church Prayer Ministry #3

Description _____

_____

Evaluation _____

_____

_____

Church Prayer Ministry #4

Description _____

_____

Evaluation _____

_____

_____

_____

Church Prayer Ministry #5

Description _____

_____

Evaluation _____

_____

_____

_____

Church Prayer Ministry #6

Description _____

_____

Evaluation _____

_____

_____

Needs and Responsibilities

Now list the prayer needs and responsibilities of your church (Needs refer to the local body, responsibilities refer to both the local and universal church). In other words, what SHOULD your church be praying for?

_____

_____

_____

_____

_____

_____

_____

_____

_____

_____

_____

_____

Brainstorm to determine some possible answers to meet these needs and responsibilities. These may include existing or potential ministries. Write down your ideas in the space provided.

_____

_____

_____

_____

_____

_____

_____

_____

_____

Spend some time now in prayer for your church and its ministry of prayer.

For Group Discussions

1. Open with a time of prayer.

2. Discuss the various prayer ministries in your church. Evaluate these ministries in light of what has been learned in this course.

3. Discuss the feasibility of starting a house of prayer for your church. If you already have a house of prayer, discuss the impact it has made upon your church.

4. List and discuss the prayer needs and responsibilities of your church.

5. Brainstorm to determine some ways in which your church might increase its prayer power.

6. Spend the remaining time in prayer. Focus on the prayer life of your church.

ASSIGNMENT: Keep praying daily. Read Chapter Nine.

Chapter Nine
Prayer & Revival

2 Chronicles 7:14: *(If)..."My people who are called by My name humble themselves and pray, and seek My face and turn from their wicked ways, then I will hear from heaven, will forgive their sin, and will heal their land."*

One of the most common desires of church leaders today is to see genuine revival take place in their midst. So many generations have passed since we have seen genuine revival that we have forgotten how revival is brought about, or even what it means.

Before we proceed, let's look at a few definitions. Revival refers to carnal Christians who have placed Christ back on the throne of their lives. This will be discussed further. Revivals are not for unbelievers. You can't revive something that never was. Evangelistic rallies or crusades are for unbelievers to hear the Gospel and have an opportunity to respond to the Gospel. Awakening refers to an outpouring of the Holy Spirit of God upon a community which includes both believers and non-believers. Believers are revived, and unbelievers are evangelized.

Many churches have been drawn into a formalistic rut where the church conducts a series of evangelistic services called a revival meeting, crusade, or rally. The results of these meetings are varied. The most common scenario finds the most faithful church members attending a progressively smaller meeting where an evangelist preaches evangelistic messages to the most devout church members. Few, if any, non-Christians are present, and very few decisions are made with the possible exception of the children of church members. Then everyone feels guilty that genuine revival did not come. But at least the attempt was made, and everyone moves on until the next annual or semi-annual revival meeting.

Vibrant praying churches experience revival or renewal on a regular basis. This becomes a normal part of church life which renews and empowers the church's evangelistic thrust.

Spiritually stagnant churches who desire revival have begun to increase their prayer efforts for revivals. Home prayer meetings and around the clock prayer vigils have become popular. While this is an improvement, it seldom accomplishes its purpose. A handful of active church members meeting in homes a couple of times does not generally bring revival. As for the prayer vigils, although it sounds extraordinary, it usually involves 24 hours of individual prayer. Look at it this way: twenty-four people praying for one hour produces more power because corporate prayer is generally more powerful than individual prayer. So if these things do not generally bring revival, how does revival come about?

Before we proceed, however, we must ask the question: "Why do we need revival?" We need revival because we have turned away from the Lordship of Jesus Christ. We have become carnal Christians, which means that we have placed ourselves back on the throne of our lives. Our primary focus and priorities relate to our personal and family goals, desires, and dreams. We want to live comfortably and to provide the best material possessions for our families more than anything else in the world.

We have forgotten, or never learned, that the primary purpose in the life of the Christian is to offer ourselves as a living sacrifice to our Lord and Savior Jesus Christ.

Romans 12:1-2: *"I urge you therefore, brethren, by the mercies of God, to present your bodies a living and holy sacrifice, acceptable to God, which is your spiritual service of worship. And do not be conformed to this world, but be transformed by the renewing of your mind, that you may prove what the will of God is, that which is good and acceptable and perfect."*

This means that our purpose in life becomes Christ's purpose in the world today. And what is that purpose? To complete Christ's mission of rescuing mankind from the Kingdom of Darkness into the Kingdom of Light. Christ's commission to Paul is to us as well:

> Acts 26:18: *"To open their eyes so that they may turn from darkness to light and from the dominion of Satan to God, in order that they may receive forgiveness of sins and an inheritance among those who have been sanctified by faith in Me."*

We are focusing on driving a new and better car, wearing the latest fashions, advancing in our job, buying new furniture, etc., while there is a life and death struggle taking place over the eternity of the souls around us, and we are literally letting them go to Hell. In the meantime, all the joys that the Holy Spirit desires to give us as we serve Christ are not available to us because we are living in the flesh. We are too decent to indulge in all the false pleasures of the world, and too worldly to claim all the joys of the Spirit. Of all mankind, we are some of the most miserable people to be found. Too many of us are the unfruitful ones spoken of by Jesus in the parable of the sower:

> Mark 4:18-19: *"And others are the ones on whom seed was sown among the thorns; these are the ones who have heard the word, and the worries of the world, and the deceitfulness of riches, and the desires for other things enter in and choke the word, and it becomes unfruitful."*

What are we seeking in revival? We are seeking to discover and claim God's will for each person and the corporate body of Christ. We need to totally sell ourselves out to become bond servants of God. We must desire to see the filling of the Holy Spirit in our lives to empower us to accomplish the will of God, and to become what God created us to become. Simply put, revival takes place when there is an outpouring of the Holy Spirit in the midst of the body of Christ.

We must also remember that Satan is at work in our churches to prevent revival from taking place. He accomplishes this by gaining a foothold in the lives of church members. Unless our people are made aware of these footholds, and claim victory over them, then genuine revival is very unlikely.

How do you bring revival about?

> 2 Chronicles 7:14: *(If...)* *"My people who are called by My name humble themselves and pray, and seek My face and turn from their wicked ways, then I will hear from heaven, will forgive their sin, and will heal their land."*

Revival comes about through concentrated, concerted, and corporate prayer. We must first recognize our need, humble ourselves before God, and pray for restoration and revival. We should pray for the Holy Spirit to move in our midst.

> Acts 4:31: *"And when they had prayed, the place where they had gathered together was shaken, and they were all filled with the Holy Spirit, and began to speak the word of God with boldness."*

Many of our people do not know how to pray. Those who do know how, are often not motivated to pray as they should. The great awakenings and revivals of the last few centuries have all been in response to movements of prayer. It generally begins when an individual or small group of people are burdened for revival and feel called of God to pray extensively for revival. The burden for revival and prayer then begins to expand in slowly, but ever increasing numbers. Those who are praying begin to be convicted of their sins by the Holy Spirit. There is much confession of sin and a turning toward God on the part of those praying.

Now back to revival. As the problem of sin is dealt with, the number of those praying increases until the majority of the church or churches are praying daily on a personal level, in small groups, and in extended corporate times of prayer. Then there is an outpouring of the Holy Spirit upon the church and the community. That is when the evangelistic thrust is made. The Holy Spirit begins to work in the lives of those in the community while the church members are boldly empowered to share the Gospel. Members are now open to new approaches to evangelism, and are willing to take their faith outside the church building. People are converted and the church brings in the harvest according to His will. Evangelistic rallies work well at this point.

Our generation has forgotten that mass meetings for evangelism are for the purpose of bringing in the harvest produced through genuine revival which begins with prayer. Without an outpouring of the Holy Spirit resulting in revival and victorious Christian living, the evangelistic meetings are often dead. These meetings are still a valid form of church evangelism, but we must learn to pray for revival and conduct our evangelistic meetings after revival has begun. It is the prayer, not meetings, that bring revival.

How can we be bring about revival? First, there must be a desire from the church leaders to see revival take place. If that desire is present, there must be an adequate biblical understanding of the role of prayer in revival. Secondly, the church and its leaders must ask the Lord to teach them and motivate them to pray. Prayer meetings for the purpose of revival must begin. As people become interested in prayer, they must be guided into a lifestyle of intercessory prayer. A time of prayer against the work of Satan in the lives of individuals may be needed, followed by repentance, and the commitment of lives to God and the working of the Holy Spirit. Thirdly, the congregation needs to grow in its corporate prayer life. Extended seasons of prayer (several hours or even through the night) and corporate days of prayer and fasting need to be conducted, pleading with God for revival to come. When revival comes, the people should go out and begin developing relationships with non-Christians. They should pray for the salvation of these people daily and pray for opportunities to discuss spiritual things. These non-Christians need to be presented with the claims of Christ and drawn into the body of Christ. If a large harvest begins, evangelistic meetings may need to be conducted.

Personal Evaluation

Pray about each question before you answer it.

Are there any areas of habitual sin (sins of the flesh, sins of the spirit, or sins of omission) in your life? Yes _____ No _____

If so, what are they?

What about the sin of prayerlessness? Yes _____   No _____

Are there any areas in your life where you have refused to allow the Holy Spirit complete control of your life?   Yes _____   No _____

If so, what are they?

Has Satan used you in any way to create dissension in your church, to hinder the work of evangelism, or to hurt a believer? Yes _____   No _____   If so, explain.

Do you have a personal need for renewal or revival in your own life? Yes _____   No _____   If so, spend some time in prayer and ask the Lord to show you what He wants you to do. Review each of the previous questions as you pray.

For Group Discussions

1. Open with a time of prayer.

2. Review the material on prayer and revival in this chapter. How were the principles taught in this chapter unknowingly followed in the testimony of revival in Chapter One?

3. How has your church historically sought revival? Based upon this chapter, what have been some of your mistakes? Brainstorm to discover ways in which your church can experience revival.

4. Discuss the personal evaluations for revival. Ask students to share with the class what they learned about themselves, including any testimonies of personal renewal.

5. If your class sessions are 90 minutes in length, consider showing the video entitled *The Role of Prayer in Spiritual Awakenings* by J. Edwin Orr.

ASSIGNMENT: Complete Chapter Ten by the next class meeting.

Chapter Ten
Prayer & Evangelism

Preparation

Prepare yourself for this session with prayer. Give praise to God, confess your sins before God, and pray for the power of the Holy Spirit to work through your life. Prepare yourself to be sensitive to the leadership of the Holy Spirit for revelation, instruction, and direction.

Prayer and Evangelism

The following is a careful study of Paul's teaching on evangelism. In this single paragraph of Scripture (Colossians 4:2-6), Paul has given us powerful instruction on how to win people to Christ.

First, read the whole passage.

> Colossians 4:2-6 *"Devote yourselves to prayer, keeping alert in it with an attitude of thanksgiving; praying at the same time for us as well, that God may open up to us a door for the word, so that we may speak forth the mystery of Christ, for which I have also been imprisoned; in order that I may make it clear in the way I ought to speak. Conduct yourselves with wisdom toward outsiders, making the most of the opportunity. Let your speech always be with grace, seasoned, as it were, with salt, so that you may know how you should respond to each person."*

Now let's carefully break down these verses to see what Paul means.

First of all, in the context of evangelism, Paul says to *Devote yourselves to prayer.* The word for *devote* means to persevere continually. Prayer and evangelism go hand in hand. If we are to take evangelism seriously, we must devote ourselves continually to prayer for the salvation of the souls God has brought into our paths.

We are also to *keep alert in it. It* refers to our prayers. As we live out our life, and in our daily walk, we should be alert to opportunities to let the light and joy of Christ shine through us. If you are alert in your prayer, before you talk to any stranger, or non-Christian acquaintance, you should utter a prayer for that person before you even say a word to them. In only a brief moment in your heart, you can pray that God would cleanse you of any sin that would be a hindrance to the work of the Holy Spirit, and pray that the Spirit would show you what to say and do so that this person might ultimately come to know Christ.

We are to pray *with an attitude of thanksgiving*. What does it mean that our evangelistic prayers should be with an attitude of thanksgiving? As we pray evangelistically, we should pray with an attitude of expectancy for what God is going to do. We should be expecting results from our witness, praying with faith that our witness will not return to us empty and without effect. Remember the continuum on faith and doubting. We should pray believing that God will work. If we do believe, then our faith will be accompanied by a prayerful attitude of thanksgiving to God for what He is doing, and is going to do.

Praying at the same time for us as well. Here Paul is instructing us to pray for one another's witness. As we pray for our own evangelistic efforts, we should also be in prayer for the witness of others in the body of Christ. The cell group (small fellowship and evangelistic groups that meet in homes) is an ideal church structure in which to evangelize and pray this way. But you can also choose to work and pray this way through home Bible studies, youth fellowships, or Sunday School classes. In small group evangelism, all of the members are praying specifically for the witness of each member, and the salvation of specific individuals.

We've been talking a lot about prayer so far, but exactly what are we praying for? For one thing, we are praying *that God may open up to us a door for the word*. God is the one who will provide the opportunity for us to witness to others. But we need to pray for those opportunities. Satan will do everything he can do to prevent these doors for the word to be opened for us. So we must do battle and pray for these opportunities. If we will pray, God will answer this prayer.

So that we may speak forth the mystery of Christ. When the door has been opened, we must pray that the mystery of Christ will be revealed through our lives and words. It is not the words that you say that will reveal the mystery of Christ. Paul speaks of the message of Christ as a mystery because the truths of the Gospel are foolishness to men. You cannot convince someone to become a Christian through your eloquent words. It is a mystery that can only be revealed through the Holy Spirit. The Holy Spirit works in our lives to show us what to say, but the Holy Spirit is also at work in the life of the unbeliever to translate what is said, convict them of their sin, reveal the truths of this mystery to them, and draw them to Christ.

For which I have also been imprisoned. Paul warns us that our witness will be opposed. There is a real battle going on over our offensive attacks upon Satan's kingdom. There is a parallel passage to Colossians 4:2-6 in Ephesians 6:18-20. Read both passages and note the striking resemblance.

How many words or phrases can you find that are similar? _____

Now read Ephesians 6:10-17. What is the context of that passage?

_____

_____

_____

_____

Evangelism, spiritual warfare, and prayer are so intertwined that it is hard to separate them. Now let's return to our study of Colossians 4:2-6.

We should also be praying that the Holy Spirit will be in complete control of our witness so that everything we say will be exactly what that person needs to hear. So we should pray *in order that I may make it clear in the way I ought to speak.* There is no one line or phrase that we should always use in our witness. Many times, we will say nothing directly about Christ. What do we say? How do we act? Only the Holy Spirit knows what that person needs to hear, so we must trust Him to work through us.

Conduct yourselves with wisdom toward outsiders. The word for *conduct* means *to walk*. This is referring to our everyday walk of life. *Outsiders* refers to non-Christians. The core of our witness for Christ is carried on in our everyday walk of life. The people we meet at work, in our neighborhood, in our leisure activities, as we shop, and where ever we go, the people we meet should be the basis of our witness for Christ. As we meet these people, we should pray for wisdom that God will use us to draw them to Christ.

Making the most of the opportunity literally means *redeeming the time*. As we meet people in our everyday walk, Paul is telling us that we should not let these opportunities be wasted. We should redeem these everyday interactions with non-Christians for the sake of the Gospel. This is the heart of our witness. Most of us waste the time we spend in the normal everyday interactions we have with the people we meet each day. Don't let that time be wasted. Redeem that time for the Gospel. The word for *time* refers to a seasonal time. There is a right time and a wrong time. There is a right time to directly proclaim Christ, and there is a wrong time. How direct or indirect should our witness be? As we go back to previous verses, we remember that the Holy Spirit knows the right thing to say and do so that our witness will be effective.

Let your speech always be with grace. As we meet non-Christians in our everyday walk, our speech should be gracious. The things we say, our body language, and our facial expressions communicate to those we meet what our true feelings toward them really are. When we pass by people in our everyday walk, particularly in the cities, we are in a hurry. We really don't care about the people we meet. As far as we are concerned, they can literally go to Hell. If we have an attitude of love, joy, and concern in our lives toward those we meet, we will certainly be noticed. And if we are demonstrating a joy and concern, hurting people will be drawn to us.

Seasoned, as it were, with salt. Our interaction with these unbelievers and our conversations with them should be seasoned with salt. There were many different uses of the word *salt* in New Testament times. The one that seems to fit here is the use of salt as fertilizer. In the context of this passage, we are sowing the seed of the Gospel. Just the right amount of salt serves as a good fertilizer for crops. This was a common practice in Jesus' day. But there was one problem with using salt in this way. If you used too much salt, the ground would become infertile and nothing would grow. It is the same way with our witness. How direct should our witness be? Should we present the plan of salvation to this stranger? Or should we speak kindly, smile, and just show our concern for them? Our presentation of God's love is just like using salt for fertilizer. If we use too much, that person will be offended and the soil of their lives will be infertile to our witness. How do we know how much to use? The Holy Spirit will show us if we will ask Him to do it.

So that you may know how you should respond to each person. This last phrase is very important. It tells us two things. First of all, we should be responding, talking, and interacting with the people we meet in our daily walk. But it also tells us that each person is unique. They have different needs, hurts, and understandings of Christianity. There is no one approach to our witness that we should use with every person. We must be sensitive to the Spirit's leading so that our witness will pierce the very heart of each unique unbeliever we meet.

In 1987, I was shopping for groceries in the state of Washington. While I was standing in the checkout line, I noticed that the checkout clerk looked extremely tired and distressed. The man at the counter was watching her very closely as if he were convinced that she was going to try and cheat him and overcharge him. The man was abrupt and rude. I began to pray for that woman. What could I do or say that could be used of God as a witness to her? I prayed that the Holy Spirit would show me what to do. When my turn came, I told her that she must have one of the toughest jobs I could think of. She looked offended and said, "What do you mean by that?" I told her I had noticed how the man had given her a difficult time and she agreed. I said, "With all those long hours of standing, with everyone in a hurry and pressing you to go faster, and with people thinking you are trying to cheat them, this must be a very difficult job." She paused, and then agreed. She said her work was very hard and that she was very tired. Then she added, "You're the first person that's ever told me they appreciate what I do and understand how hard this job is." She smiled and said, "That really means a lot. Thanks."

The next time I went shopping, I looked to find that same lady. She was there and I got in her checkout line. She looked tired and distressed as before. When she noticed me out of the corner of her eye, a smile came across her face. I don't remember what I said to her, but I gave her a word of encouragement and told her that I had been praying for her. I never saw that woman again, but I believe that some seed was sown that God has used.

I use this illustration as an example of the principles described in this verse. The time we spend to check out our groceries is a good example of wasted time that needs to be redeemed for the Gospel.

As you study this passage, note the dependence of our witness upon prayer, the Holy Spirit, and our availability. Now reread this passage with new understanding.

> Colossians 4:2-6 *"Devote yourselves to prayer, keeping alert in it with an attitude of thanksgiving; praying at the same time for us as well, that God may open up to us a door for the word, so that we may speak forth the mystery of Christ, for which I have also been imprisoned; in order that I may make it clear in the way I ought to speak. Conduct yourselves with wisdom toward outsiders, making the most of the opportunity. Let your speech always be with grace, seasoned, as it were, with salt, so that you may know how you should respond to each person."*

It is thrilling to practice the principles Paul gives us in this passage. How do you measure up to Paul's instruction?

Personal Evaluation

Answer the following questions based upon what you have learned in this chapter.

1. When you meet people during the day, are you praying and thinking about their salvation?

2. When people meet you, do they see the love and joy of Christ in your life? Explain.

3. Think of the last person you met, whom you have no idea as to whether or not they were a Christian. Based upon the material in this chapter, evaluate your interaction with that person.

4. What are some concrete ways you can implement what you have just learned as a part of your daily life?

5. Try to practice what you have learned for one full day. At the end of that day, write a diary of what happened. Was anything different in your life? Was anything different in the way people responded to you?

How I Learned to Pray for the Lost

Note: *This is an article reprinted by permission from* Alliance Life *magazine (formerly* The Alliance Witness*), the publication of The Christian and Missionary Alliance. This article gives excellent instruction in how to pray for the lost.*

Here is a remarkable testimony which should be of real help to many church planters. Since the nature of the testimony is personal, the writer requested that her name be withheld.

The letter accompanying this testimony says in part: "This is the result of my search for the right way of praying for the unsaved. I have found it to produce amazing results in a very short time. After more than twenty years of fruitless praying, it seemed that there was no possible chance for my loved ones to ever return to the faith. But after only a few weeks of the type of praying that I have outlined here I have seen them studying the Bible by the hour and attending every church service possible. Also, their whole attitude toward Christianity has changed, and all resistance seems to be gone. I have taken my place of authority in Christ and am using it against the Enemy. I have not looked at myself to see if I am fit or not; I have just taken my place and have prayed that the Holy Spirit may do His convicting work. If each and every member of the Body of Christ would do this, what a change would be made in this world!"

Believers everywhere are burdened for unsaved or backsliding loved ones. However, many are praying in the spirit of fear and worry instead of in faith.

This has caused me to seek for definite light on how to pray, feeling the need of praying the right prayer and also the need for a definite promise or word from God on which to base my faith when praying for the unsaved. Praise God--He never fails to give such needed help.

Perhaps because the salvation of some seemed to me to be an impossibility, the first verse of Scripture that was given to me was Mark 10:27, *"With God all things are possible."* (KJV).

The next Scripture verse had occupied my attention for some time, but it took on a new meaning: "*(For the weapons of our warfare are not carnal, but mighty through God to the pulling down of strongholds;) casting down imaginations [speculations] and every high thing that exalteth itself against the knowledge of God and bringing into captivity every thought to the obedience of Christ,"* (II Cor. 10:4,5 KJV). This shows the mighty power of our spiritual weapons. We must pray that all of this will be accomplished in the ones for whom we are concerned; that is, that the works of the Enemy will be torn down.

Finally, I was given the solid foundation for my prayers --the basis of redemption. In reality, Christ's redemption purchased all mankind, so that we may say that each one is actually God's purchased possession, although he is still held by the Enemy. We must, through the prayer of faith, claim and take for God in the name of the Lord Jesus that which is rightfully His. This can be done only on the basis of redemption. This is not meant to imply that, because all persons have been purchased by God through redemption, they are automatically saved. They must believe and accept the Gospel for themselves; our intercession enables them to do this.

To pray in the name of the Lord Jesus is to ask for, or to claim, the things which the blood of Christ has secured. Therefore, each individual for whom prayer is made should be claimed by name as God's purchased possession, in the name of the Lord Jesus and on the basis of His shed blood.

We should claim the tearing down of all works of Satan, such as false doctrine, unbelief, atheistic teaching, and hatred, which the Enemy may have built up in their thinking. We must pray that their very thoughts will be brought into captivity to the obedience of Christ.

With the authority of the name of the Lord Jesus, we must claim their deliverance from the power and persuasion of the Evil One and from the love of the world and the lust of the flesh. We should also pray that their conscience may be convicted, that God may bring them to the point of repentance, and that they may listen and believe as they hear or read the Word of God. Our prayer must be that God's will and purposes may be accomplished in and through them.

Intercession must be persistent--not to persuade God, for redemption is by God, but because of the Enemy. Our prayer and resistance are against the enemy--the awful powers and rulers of darkness. It is our duty before God to fight for the souls for whom Christ died. Just as some must preach to them the good news of redemption, others must fight the powers of darkness on their behalf through prayer.

Satan yields only what and when he must, and he renews his attacks in subtle ways. Therefore, prayer must be definite and persistent, even long after definite results are seen. And we must pray for the new Christian even after he begins to be established in the faith.

We will find that as we pray, the Holy Spirit will give new directions. At one time I was interceding for a soul and began to feel that my prayers were largely ineffective. Then the Holy Spirit inspired me to begin presenting that person to God in the name of the Lord Jesus. As I obeyed this leading, praying, "I present so-and-so to God in the name of the Lord Jesus," I felt that my prayers were gradually becoming more effective. It seemed that I was drawing that person from deep within the very camp of the enemy. Then I was able to proceed as usual, claiming every detail of that life for God, using the power of the blood against the enemy. This is true warfare in the spiritual realm. Thank God that our spiritual weapons are might and that our authority in Christ is far above all the authority of the rulers, powers, and forces of darkness, so that the enemy must yield. But it takes faith and patience and persistence.

Missionaries on foreign and home fields can resist the enemy in their districts, communities, and schools by using the power of the blood of Jesus against the powers of darkness, sin, and unbelief. With the authority of the name of the Lord Jesus they can demand that the enemy retreat.

Note that "*it is the spirit that quickeneth; the flesh profiteth nothing*", (John 6:63 KJV) and that "*the letter killeth, but the spirit giveth life,*" (II Cor. 3:6 KJV). Therefore, we must constantly seek the motivation of the Holy Spirit in our hearts, in our faith, in our prayers, and in our testimony. It is most important also that we confess our own sins and have them forgiven. The enemy will use every possible means to silence our intercession and to block our attack against him. We must not only understand our Enemy, our authority in Christ, and how to use our spiritual weapons but also how to wear the armor that God has provided for our protection. Thus equipped and protected, we need not have any fear. But let us always remember that we have no power and no authority other than that of Christ.

"*Now thanks be unto God, which always causeth us to triumph in Christ,*" (II Cor. 2:14 KJV). "*Greater is he that is in you, than he that is in the world,*" (I John 4:4 KJV). (End of article)

Conclusion

When you are praying for someone's salvation, include the following areas in your prayers:

1. Present the person by name to Jesus Christ as His purchased possession.

2. Pray against the powers of darkness that claim a hold on this person's life so that this person will have the freedom to choose to accept or reject Jesus Christ apart from Satan's interference or bondage.

3. Pray that the Holy Spirit will draw this person toward Christ, convict them of their sin, and reveal to them the truth of God's plan for salvation.

4. Pray that God will bring circumstances, people, and events into this person's life in order to reveal to them their need for Christ.

5. Pray that God will use you as an instrument to bring this person to Christ. Pray that the Holy Spirit will guide your every word and deed so that you will say and do the right thing at the right time. Pray that the light and joy of Christ will shine through your life as a testimony of the Christian faith.

For Group Discussions

1. Open with a time of prayer.

2. Review the material on Colossians 4:2-6.

3. For each question of the personal evaluation, ask class members to share what they learned about themselves.

4. Review the material on how to pray for the lost. Stress the importance of keeping unbelievers on our daily prayer lists. Give students the opportunity to add the names of unbelievers to their prayer lists.

5. Spend the remaining time in prayer. Pray for the salvation of specific unbelievers and for opportunities to share Christ with them as appropriate.

Appendix A - Resources

This appendix includes possible periodical resources for creating prayer lists.

African Report. 833 United Nations Plaza, New York, NY 10017.

Alliance Life. Christian and Missionary Alliance, Box 35000, Colorado Springs, CO 80935-3500.

Asian Report. Asian Outreach International, G.P.O., Box 3448, Hong Kong.

Breakthrough. News of the Soviet Union, Eastern Europe and the Slavic World. Box 1122, Wheaton, IL 60189.

Church Around the World. Prayer Newsheet (5 1/2" by 8 1/2") published by Tyndale House Publishers, Inc., 351 Executive Drive, Carol Stream, IL 60188.

The Commission. A magazine of the SBC Foreign Mission Board, P.O. Box 6767, Richmond, VA 23230.

The Europe Report. Greater Europe Mission. Box 668 Wheaton, IL 60189.

East Asia's Millions. Overseas Missionary Fellowship, 10 West Dry Creek Circle, Littleton, CO 80120-4413.

Latin American Evangelist. P.O. Box 52-7900, Miami, FL 33152-7900.

Mission Frontiers. Bulletin of the U.S. Center for World Mission. 1605 Elizabeth St., Pasadena, CA 91104.

Reimer, Johannes. *Operation Soviet Union*. A prayer guide avalaible through Logos, P.O. Box 409, Fresno, CA 93708-0409.

Johnstone, Patrick. *Operation World*. A Christian encyclopedia of the world with prayer requests and other information on each country. Published by WEC International and Send The Light.

Partners in Missions. A guide to Southern Baptist Foreign Missions. Available through the Foreign Mission Board, P.O. Box 6767, Richmond, VA 23230.

Royal Service. A magazine of the Southern Baptist Woman's Missionary Union.

SIM Now. 1236 Arrow Pine Dr., Charlotte, NC 28217.

World Christian. P.O. Box 70052, Pasadena, CA 91107.

World Evangelism. 1 Maritime Square, #12-06, World Trade Center, Singapore 0409.

World Mission Journal. A periodical of the Brotherhood Commission of the Southern Baptist Convention.

World Vision. 919 W. Huntington Dr., Monrovia CA 91016.

Other Periodicals (List others related to your church)

Books

Bounds, E.M. *Power Through Prayer.*

Duewel, Wesley L. *Mighty Prevailing Prayer* and *Touch The World Through Prayer.*

Hallesby, O. A. *Prayer.*

Hunt and Walker. *The Prayer Life.*

Murray, Andrew. *The Prayer Life* and *With Christ in the School of Prayer.*

Parks, Helen Jean. *Holding the Ropes.*

Taylor, Jack. *Prayer: Life's Limitless Reach.*

Taylor, Mrs. Howard. *Behind The Ranges.*

Others:

Appendix B - Prayer Lists

The prayer lists may be photocopied to create your prayer notebook. There is a 5 1/2" by 8 1/2" format and a smaller 3" by 5" format.

PRAYER CHECKLIST

PRAISE and THANKSGIVING

CONFESSION: Flesh, Spirit, Omission, Unconscious

SPIRITUAL PREPARATION
Filling of the Spirit
Dear Heavenly Father, fill me with your Holy Spirit today.
Fruit of the Spirit. Pray Galatians 5:22.
Bear the fruit of Your Spirit in my life today. The fruit of love..., joy..., peace..., patience..., kindness..., goodness..., gentleness..., faithfulness..., and self-control...
Christ in Me. Pray Galatians 2:20.
Dear Father, I want to claim today that I am crucified with Christ, it is no longer I who live, but Christ lives in me. And the life I now live in the flesh this day, I live by faith in the Son of God, who loves me and delivered Himself up for me.
Claim Romans 8:28.
I want to claim Your promise today that all things work together for good to those who love You, to those called according to Your purpose. I love You Lord and pray that I will be in the center of Your will today.
Protection from Satan.
Protect me and my family from the Evil One today. The Lord rebuke you Satan!
Thy Kingdom come.
Dear Father, I pray for the second coming of Christ, for A.D. 2000, Bold Mission Thrust, and other efforts that every person on earth will hear the Good News of Christ by the year 2000.

PRAYER LISTS

OPERATION WORLD

PRAYERFUL SCRIPTURE READING

PRAYERFUL MEDITATION

FAMILY PRAYER

PRAYER WITHOUT CEASING

Prayer for a country
WITHOUT Mission Work

Name of Country _____

No. Date Prayer Requests

Date Answered

1. (/   ) _____

Prayer for a country
WITH Mission Work

Name of Country _____

No. Date Prayer Requests   Date Answered

1. (/) _____

_____

_____

_____

_____

_____

_____

_____

_____

_____

_____

_____

_____

_____

_____

_____

_____

_____

_____

_____

_____

_____

_____

_____

Prayer for Missionaries, Agencies, & Workers

No. Date Prayer Requests

Date Answered

1. (/)

_____

_____

_____

_____

_____

_____

_____

_____

_____

_____

_____

_____

_____

_____

_____

_____

_____

_____

_____

_____

_____

_____

_____

_____

Prayer for Church Staff & Leaders

No. Date Prayer Requests

Date Answered

1. (/   )

Prayer for Family & Friends

No. Date Prayer Requests

Date Answered

1. (/   )

Personal Petitions

No. Date Prayer Requests

Date Answered

1. (/)

Other Prayer Items

No. Date Prayer Requests   Date Answered

1. (/   )

PRAYER CHECKLIST

- PRAISE and THANKSGIVING
- CONFESSION: Flesh, Spirit, Omission, Unconscious
- SPIRITUAL PREPARATION

Filling of the Spirit

Dear Heavenly Father, fill me with your Holy Spirit today.

Fruit of the Spirit. Pray Galatians 5:22.

Bear the fruit of Your Spirit in my life today. The fruit of love..., joy..., peace..., patience..., kindness..., goodness..., gentleness..., faithfulness..., and self-control...

Christ in Me. Pray Galatians 2:20.

Dear Father, I want to claim today that I am crucified with Christ, it is no longer I who live, but Christ lives in me. And the life I now live in the flesh this day, I live by faith in the Son of God, who loves me and delivered Himself up for me.

Claim Romans 8:28.

I want to claim Your promise today that all things work together for good to those who love You, to those called according to Your purpose. I love You Lord and pray that I will be in the center of Your will today.

Protection from Satan.

Protect me and my family from the Evil One today. The Lord rebuke you Satan!

Thy Kingdom come.

Dear Father, I pray for the second coming of Christ, for A.D. 2000, Bold Mission Thrust, and other efforts that every person on earth will hear the Good News of Christ by the year 2000.

- PRAYER LISTS
- *OPERATION WORLD*
- PRAYERFUL SCRIPTURE READING
- PRAYERFUL MEDITATION
- PRAYER WITHOUT CEASING

Prayer for a country
WITHOUT Mission Work

Name of Country _____

No. Date Prayer Requests   Date Answered

1. (/   ) _____

_____

_____

_____

_____

_____

_____

_____

_____

_____

_____

_____

_____

_____

_____

_____

_____

Prayer for a country
WITH Mission Work

Name of Country _____

No. Date Prayer Requests   Date Answered

1. (/) _____

_____

_____

_____

_____

_____

_____

_____

_____

_____

_____

_____

_____

_____

_____

_____

_____

_____

Prayer for Missionaries, Agencies, & Workers

No. Date Prayer Requests   Date Answered

1. (/   ) _____

_____

_____

_____

_____

_____

_____

_____

_____

_____

_____

_____

_____

_____

_____

_____

_____

_____

_____

Prayer for Church Staff & Leaders

No. Date Prayer Requests   Date Answered

1. (/   )
_____
_____
_____
_____
_____
_____
_____
_____
_____
_____
_____
_____
_____
_____
_____
_____
_____
_____

Prayer for Family & Friends

No. Date Prayer Requests   Date Answered

1. (/   )

Personal Petitions

No. Date Prayer Requests   Date Answered

1. (/)

Other Prayer Items

No. Date Prayer Requests   Date Answered

1. (/   )

Appendix C - Note to Missionaries

Since your ministry will never grow beyond the power of the prayer behind it, it is extremely important that as many people as possible are praying daily for the specific needs of your work. It is also important that the people who are praying have a powerful prayer life and understand that mission work is a spiritual battle empowered through intercessory prayer.

Through my experience on the mission field, and conversations with missionaries throughout the world, it is all too common to find our prayer support severely lacking. Often we find ourselves so busy in ministry (working in the flesh, i.e. human activities), our own prayer lives may be lacking. We also find it difficult to produce prayer letters on a regular basis to solicit the prayer support we need. Both problems can result in powerless and fruitless ministry.

The other problem comes when we send out prayer letters to churches where they are passed out during prayer services and then are left in the pews. Others receive them and read them as a matter . of information. A few will pause and pray for us before throwing them away or sticking them in their Bibles. Such scenarios can also result in powerless and fruitless ministry.

This book has been written to help you build a powerful intercessory prayer life, and for you to send to your prayer supporters so that their prayer lives will be faithful and powerful. This book is designed to change attitudes about prayer, provide an understanding of intercessory prayer, produce a commitment to pray, and leave people praying. It also gets prayer lives organized. If your prayer supporters use their prayer notebooks, you can regularly send prayer requests in 3" by 5" and 5 1/2" by 8 1/2" formats and be assured that your prayer partners will 'pop' them into their prayer notebooks and pray for your needs on a daily basis.

TABS

DAILY

Monday

Tuesday

Wednesday

Thursday

Friday

Saturday

Sunday